Travel phrasebooks collection
«Everything Will Be Okay!»

PHRASEBOOK

- ARMENIAN -

By Andrey Taranov

THE MOST IMPORTANT PHRASES

This phrasebook contains the most important phrases and questions for basic communication
Everything you need to survive overseas

Phrasebook + 3000-word dictionary

English-Armenian phrasebook & topical vocabulary

By Andrey Taranov

The collection of "Everything Will Be Okay" travel phrasebooks published by T&P Books is designed for people traveling abroad for tourism and business. The phrasebooks contain what matters most - the essentials for basic communication. This is an indispensable set of phrases to "survive" while abroad.

This book also includes a small topical vocabulary that contains roughly 3,000 of the most frequently used words. Another section of the phrasebook provides a gastronomical dictionary that may help you order food at a restaurant or buy groceries at the store.

T&P Books Publishing
www.tpbooks.com

ISBN: 978-1-78492-457-7

This book is also available in E-book formats.
Please visit www.tpbooks.com or the major online bookstores.

FOREWORD

The collection of "Everything Will Be Okay" travel phrasebooks published by T&P Books is designed for people traveling abroad for tourism and business. The phrasebooks contain what matters most - the essentials for basic communication. This is an indispensable set of phrases to "survive" while abroad.

This phrasebook will help you in most cases where you need to ask something, get directions, find out how much something costs, etc. It can also resolve difficult communication situations where gestures just won't help.

This book contains a lot of phrases that have been grouped according to the most relevant topics. The edition also includes a small vocabulary that contains roughly 3,000 of the most frequently used words. Another section of the phrasebook provides a gastronomical dictionary that may help you order food at a restaurant or buy groceries at the store.

Take "Everything Will Be Okay" phrasebook with you on the road and you'll have an irreplaceable traveling companion who will help you find your way out of any situation and teach you to not fear speaking with foreigners.

TABLE OF CONTENTS

T&P Books Publishing

PRONUNCIATION

Letter	Armenian example	T&P phonetic alphabet	English example

Vowels

Letter	Armenian example	T&P phonetic alphabet	English example
ա	սագ	[ɑ]	shorter than in park, card
ե [1]	ելակ	[e]	elm, medal
ե [2]	մեխակ	[ɛ]	man, bad
է	էժան	[ɛ]	man, bad
ի	միս	[i]	shorter than in feet
ո [3]	ոզնի	[vɔ]	divorce, to avoid
ո [4]	բողոքել	[o]	pod, John
ու	թռչուն	[u]	book
օ [5]	օգտվել	[o]	pod, John
ը	ընտրել	[ə]	driver, teacher

Consonants

Letter	Armenian example	T&P phonetic alphabet	English example
բ	բարձր	[b]	baby, book
գ	գագաթ	[g]	game, gold
դ	դերանուն	[d]	day, doctor
զ	զվարճանալ	[z]	zebra, please
թ	թև	[th]	don't have
ժ	ժամացույց	[ʒ]	forge, pleasure
լ	լվացվել	[l]	lace, people
խ	ախտորոշում	[ɦ], [χ]	as in Scots loch
ծ	ծիածան	[ʦ]	cats, tsetse fly
կ	փակել	[k]	clock, kiss
հ	նիհարել	[h]	home, have
ձ	ծանրաձող	[ʣ]	beads, kids
ղ	մեղք	[ɣ]	between [g] and [h]
ճ	ճահիճ	[ʧ]	church, French
մ	ամայի	[m]	magic, milk
յ	նայել	[j]	yes, New York
ն	կանգառ	[n]	name, normal
շ	շուն	[ʃ]	machine, shark
չ	կրակայրիչ	[ʧh]	hitchhiker
պ	ամպ	[p]	pencil, private

Letter	Armenian example	T&P phonetic alphabet	English example
ջ	զիջել	[ʤ]	joke, general
ռ	տառ	[r]	rice, radio
ս	մաս	[s]	city, boss
վ	ավլել	[v]	very, river
տ	պատուհան	[t]	tourist, trip
ր	կարել	[r]	soft [r]
ց	բաց	[tsh]	let's handle it
փ	սարսափ	[ph]	top hat
ք	դեմք	[k]	clock, kiss
ֆ	ասֆալտ	[f]	face, food

Comments

[1] at the beginning of a word
[2] in the middle
[3] at the beginning of a word
[4] in the middle
[5] at the beginning of a word usually

LIST OF ABBREVIATIONS

English abbreviations

ab.	-	about
adj	-	adjective
adv	-	adverb
anim.	-	animate
as adj	-	attributive noun used as adjective
e.g.	-	for example
etc.	-	et cetera
fam.	-	familiar
fem.	-	feminine
form.	-	formal
inanim.	-	inanimate
masc.	-	masculine
math	-	mathematics
mil.	-	military
n	-	noun
pl	-	plural
pron.	-	pronoun
sb	-	somebody
sing.	-	singular
sth	-	something
v aux	-	auxiliary verb
vi	-	intransitive verb
vi, vt	-	intransitive, transitive verb
vt	-	transitive verb

Armenian punctuation

՜	-	Exclamation mark
՞	-	Question mark
,	-	Comma

ARMENIAN PHRASEBOOK

This section contains important phrases that may come in handy in various real-life situations.
The phrasebook will help you ask for directions, clarify a price, buy tickets, and order food at a restaurant

T&P Books Publishing

PHRASEBOOK CONTENTS

T&P Books Publishing

The bare minimum

Excuse me, …	**Ներեցեք, …** [nerets'eq, …]
Hello.	**Բարև Ձեզ:** [bar'ev dzez]
Thank you.	**Շնորհակալություն:** [shnorhakaluty'un]
Good bye.	**Ցտեսություն:** [tstesuty'un]
Yes.	**Այո:** [ay'o]
No.	**Ոչ:** [voch]
I don't know.	**Ես չգիտեմ:** [yes chgit'em]
Where? | Where to? | When?	**Ո՞րտեղ: Ո՞ւր: Ե՞րբ:** [vort'egh? ur? yerb?]
I need …	**Ինձ հարկավոր է …** [indz harkav'or e …]
I want …	**Ես ուզում եմ …** [yes uz'um em …]
Do you have …?	**Դուք ունե՞ք …:** [duq un'eq …?]
Is there a … here?	**Այստեղ կա՞ …:** [ayst'egh ka …?]
May I …?	**Ես կարո՞ղ եմ …:** [yes kar'ogh em …?]
…, please (polite request)	**Խնդրում եմ** [khndrum em]
I'm looking for …	**Ես փնտրում եմ …** [yes pntrum am …]
restroom	**զուգարան** [zugar'an]
ATM	**բանկոմատ** [bankom'at]
pharmacy (drugstore)	**դեղատուն** [deghat'un]
hospital	**հիվանդանոց** [hivandan'ots]
police station	**ոստիկանության բաժանմունք** [vostikanuty'an bazhanm'unq]
subway	**մետրո** [metr'o]

taxi	**տաքսի** [tax'i]
train station	**կայարան** [kayar'an]
My name is …	**Իմ անունը … է:** [im an'uny … e]
What's your name?	**Ձեր անունն ի՞նչ է:** [dzer an'unn inch e?]
Could you please help me?	**Օգնեցեք ինձ, խնդրեմ:** [ognets'eq indz, khndrem]
I've got a problem.	**Ես խնդիր ունեմ:** [yes khndir un'em]
I don't feel well.	**Ես ինձ վատ եմ զգում:** [yes indz vat am zgum]
Call an ambulance!	**Շտապ օգնություն կանչեք:** [shtap ognuty'un kanch'eq!]
May I make a call?	**Կարո՞ղ եմ զանգահարել:** [kar'ogh am zangahar'el?]
I'm sorry.	**Ներեցեք** [nerets'eq]
You're welcome.	**Խնդրեմ** [kndrem]
I, me	**ես** [yes]
you (inform.)	**դու** [du]
he	**նա** [na]
she	**նա** [na]
they (masc.)	**նրանք** [nrank]
they (fem.)	**նրանք** [nrank]
we	**մենք** [menq]
you (pl)	**դուք** [duq]
you (sg, form.)	**Դուք** [duq]
ENTRANCE	**ՄՈՒՏՔ** [mutq]
EXIT	**ԵԼՔ** [yelq]
OUT OF ORDER	**ՉԻ ԱՇԽԱՏՈՒՄ** [chi ashkhat'um]
CLOSED	**ՓԱԿ Է** [pak e]

OPEN	ԲԱՑ Է [bats e]
FOR WOMEN	ԿԱՆԱՆՑ ՀԱՄԱՐ [kan'ants ham'ar]
FOR MEN	ՏՂԱՄԱՐԴԿԱՆՑ ՀԱՄԱՐ [tghamardk'ants ham'ar]

Questions

Where?	**Որտե՞ղ:** [vort'egh?]
Where to?	**Ո՞ւր:** [ur?]
Where from?	**Որտեղի՞ց:** [vortegh'its?]
Why?	**Ինչո՞ւ:** [inch'u?]
For what reason?	**Ինչի՞ համար:** [inch'i ham'ar?]
When?	**Ե՞րբ:** [yerb?]
How long?	**Ինչքա՞ն ժամանակ:** [inchq'an zhaman'ak?]
At what time?	**Ժամը քանիսի՞ն:** [zh'amy qanis'in?]
How much?	**Ի՞նչ արժե:** [inch arzh'e?]
Do you have ...?	**Դուք ունե՞ք ...:** [duq un'eq ...?]
Where is ...?	**Որտե՞ղ է գտնվում ...:** [vort'egh e gtnvum ...?]
What time is it?	**Ժամը քանի՞սն է:** [zh'amy qan'isn e?]
May I make a call?	**Կարո՞ղ եմ զանգահարել:** [kar'ogh am zangahar'el?]
Who's there?	**Ո՞վ է:** [ov e?]
Can I smoke here?	**Կարո՞ղ եմ այստեղ ծխել:** [kar'ogh am ayst'egh tskhel?]
May I ...?	**Ես կարո՞ղ եմ ...:** [yes kar'ogh em ...?]

Needs

I'd like ...	**Ես կուզենայի ...** [yes kuzen'ayi ...]
I don't want ...	**Ես չեմ ուզում ...** [yes chem uz'um ...]
I'm thirsty.	**Ես ծարավ եմ:** [yes tsar'av am]
I want to sleep.	**Ես ուզում եմ քնել:** [yes uz'um am qnel]
I want ...	**Ես ուզում եմ ...** [yes uz'um am ...]
to wash up	**լվացվել** [lvatsv'el]
to brush my teeth	**ատամներս մաքրել** [atamn'ers maqr'el]
to rest a while	**մի քիչ հանգստանալ** [mi qich hangstan'al]
to change my clothes	**շորերս փոխել** [shor'ers pokh'el]
to go back to the hotel	**վերադառնալ հյուրանոց** [veradarn'al hyuran'ots]
to buy ...	**գնել ...** [gnel ...]
to go to ...	**գնալ ...** [gnal ...]
to visit ...	**այցելել ...** [aytsel'el ...]
to meet with ...	**հանդիպել ... հետ** [handip'el ... het]
to make a call	**զանգահարել** [zangahar'el]
I'm tired.	**Ես հոգնել եմ:** [yes hogn'el am]
We are tired.	**Մենք հոգնել ենք:** [menq hogn'el enq]
I'm cold.	**Ես մրսում եմ:** [yes mrsum am]
I'm hot.	**Ես շոգում եմ:** [yes shog'um am]
I'm OK.	**Ես լավ եմ:** [yes lav am]

I need to make a call.	**Ես պետք է զանգահարեմ:** [yes petq e zangahar'em]
I need to go to the restroom.	**Ես զուգարան եմ ուզում:** [yes zugar'an am uz'um]
I have to go.	**Գնալուս ժամանակն է:** [gnal'us zhaman'akn e]
I have to go now.	**Ես պետք է գնամ:** [yes petq e gnam]

Asking for directions

Excuse me, ...	**Ներեցեք, ...** [nerets'eq, ...]
Where is ...?	**Որտե՞ղ է գտնվում ...** [vort'egh e gtnvum ...?]
Which way is ...?	**Ո՞ր ուղղությամբ է գտնվում ...** [vor ughghuty'amb e gtnv'um ...?]
Could you help me, please?	**Օգնեցեք ինձ, խնդրեմ:** [ognets'eq indz, khndrem]
I'm looking for ...	**Ես փնտրում եմ ...** [yes pntrum am ...]
I'm looking for the exit.	**Ես փնտրում եմ ելքը:** [yes pntrum am y'elky]
I'm going to ...	**Ես գնում եմ ...** [yes gnum am ...]
Am I going the right way to ...?	**Ես ճի՞շտ եմ գնում ...:** [yes chisht am gnum ...?]
Is it far?	**Դա հեռո՞ւ է:** [da her'u e?]
Can I get there on foot?	**Ես կհասնե՞մ այնտեղ ոտքով:** [yes khasn'em aynt'egh votq'ov?]
Can you show me on the map?	**Ցույց տվեք ինձ քարտեզի վրա, խնդրում եմ:** [tsuyts tveq indz qartez'i vra, khndrum am]
Show me where we are right now.	**Ցույց տվեք՝ որտեղ ենք մենք հիմա:** [tsuyts tveq vort'egh enk menq him'a]
Here	**Այստեղ** [ayst'egh]
There	**Այնտեղ** [aynt'egh]
This way	**Այստեղ** [ayst'egh]
Turn right.	**Թեքվեք աջ:** [tekv'ek aj]
Turn left.	**Թեքվեք ձախ:** [tekv'ek dzakh]
first (second, third) turn	**առաջին (երկրորդ, երրորդ) շրջադարձ** [araj'in (yerkr'ord, err'ord) shrjad'ardz]
to the right	**դեպի աջ** [dep'i aj]

to the left	**դեպի ձախ** [dep'i dzakh]
Go straight.	**Գնացեք ուղիղ:** [gnats'ek ugh'igh]

Signs

WELCOME!	ԲԱՐԻ՜ ԳԱԼՈՒՍՏ: [bar'i gal'ust!]
ENTRANCE	ՄՈՒՏՔ [mutq]
EXIT	ԵԼՔ [yelq]
PUSH	ԴԵՊԻ ՆԵՐՍ [dep'i ners]
PULL	ԴԵՊԻ ԴՈՒՐՍ [dep'i durs]
OPEN	ԲԱՑ Է [bats e]
CLOSED	ՓԱԿ Է [pak e]
FOR WOMEN	ԿԱՆԱՆՑ ՀԱՄԱՐ [kan'ants ham'ar]
FOR MEN	ՏՂԱՄԱՐԴԿԱՆՑ ՀԱՄԱՐ [tghamardk'ants ham'ar]
MEN, GENTS	ՏՂԱՄԱՐԴԿԱՆՑ ԶՈՒԳԱՐԱՆ [tghamardk'ants zugar'an]
WOMEN, LADIES	ԿԱՆԱՆՑ ԶՈՒԳԱՐԱՆ [kan'ants zugar'an]
DISCOUNTS	ԶԵՂՉ [zeghch]
SALE	ԻՍՊԱՌ ՎԱՃԱՌՔ [isp'ar vach'ark]
FREE	ԱՆՎՃԱՐ [anvch'ar]
NEW!	ՆՈՐՈ՛ՒՅԹ [nor'uyt]
ATTENTION!	ՈՒՇԱԴՐՈՒԹՅՈ՛ՒՆ [ushadruty'un]
NO VACANCIES	ԱԶԱՏ ՀԱՄԱՐՆԵՐ ՉԿԱՆ [az'at hamarn'er chk'an]
RESERVED	ՊԱՏՎԻՐՎԱԾ Է [patvirv'ats e]
ADMINISTRATION	ԱԴՄԻՆԻՍՏՐԱՑԻԱ [administratsi'a]
STAFF ONLY	ՄԻԱՅՆ ԱՆՁՆԱԿԱԶՄԻ ՀԱՄԱՐ [mi'ayn andznakazm'i ham'ar]

BEWARE OF THE DOG!	ԿԱՏԱՂԱԾ ՇՈՒՆ [katagh'ats shun]
NO SMOKING!	ՉԾԽԵ՛Լ [chtskh'el]
DO NOT TOUCH!	ՁԵՌՔԵՐՈՎ ՉԴԻՊՉԵԼ [dzerkyer'ov chdipch'el]
DANGEROUS	ՎՏԱՆԳԱՎՈՐ Է [vtangav'or e]
DANGER	ՎՏԱՆԳ [vtang]
HIGH VOLTAGE	ԲԱՐՁՐ ԼԱՐՈՒՄ [bardzr lar'um]
NO SWIMMING!	ԼՈՂԱԼՆ ԱՐԳԵԼՎՈՒՄ Է [logh'aln argelv'um e]

OUT OF ORDER	ՉԻ ԱՇԽԱՏՈՒՄ [chi ashkhat'um]
FLAMMABLE	ԴՅՈՒՐԱՎԱՌ Է [dyurav'ar e]
FORBIDDEN	ԱՐԳԵԼՎԱԾ Է [argelv'ats e]
NO TRESPASSING!	ՄՈՒՏՔՆ ԱՐԳԵԼՎԱԾ Է [mutkn argelv'ats e]
WET PAINT	ՆԵՐԿՎԱԾ Է [nerkv'ats e]

CLOSED FOR RENOVATIONS	ՓԱԿՎԱԾ Է ՎԵՐԱՆՈՐՈԳՄԱՆ [pakv'ats e veranorogm'an]
WORKS AHEAD	ՎԵՐԱՆՈՐՈԳՄԱՆ ԱՇԽԱՏԱՆՔՆԵՐ [veranorogm'an ashkhatankn'er]
DETOUR	ՇՐՋԱՆՑՈՒՄ [shrjants'um]

Transportation. General phrases

plane	**ինքնաթիռ** [inqnat'ir]
train	**գնացք** [gnatsq]
bus	**ավտոբուս** [avtob'us]
ferry	**լաստանավ** [lastanav]
taxi	**տաքսի** [tax'i]
car	**ավտոմեքենա** [avtomeqen'a]
schedule	**չվացուցակ** [chvatsuts'ak]
Where can I see the schedule?	**Որտե՞ղ կարելի է նայել չվացուցակը:** [vort'egh karel'i e nay'el chvatsuts'aky?]
workdays (weekdays)	**աշխատանքային օրեր** [ashkhatankay'in or'er]
weekends	**հանգստյան օրեր** [hangsty'an or'er]
holidays	**տոնական օրեր** [tonak'an or'er]
DEPARTURE	**ՄԵԿՆՈՒՄ** [mekn'um]
ARRIVAL	**ԺԱՄԱՆՈՒՄ** [zhaman'um]
DELAYED	**ՈՒՇԱՑՈՒՄ** [ushats'um]
CANCELED	**ՉԵՂՅԱԼ** [cheghy'al]
next (train, etc.)	**հաջորդ** [haj'ord]
first	**առաջին** [araj'in]
last	**վերջին** [verj'in]
When is the next ...?	**Ե՞րբ է լինելու հաջորդ ...:** [yerb e linel'u haj'ordy ...?]
When is the first ...?	**Ե՞րբ է մեկնում առաջին ...:** [yerb e mekn'um araj'in ...?]

When is the last …?	**Ե՞րբ է մեկնում վերջին …:** [yerb e mekn'um verj'in …?]
transfer (change of trains, etc.)	**նստափոխ** [nstap'okh]
to make a transfer	**նստափոխ կատարել** [nstap'okh katar'el]
Do I need to make a transfer?	**Ես պետք է նստափո՞խ կատարեմ:** [yes petq e nstap'okh katar'em?]

Buying tickets

Where can I buy tickets?	**Որտե՞ղ կարող եմ տոմսեր գնել:** [vort'egh kar'ogh am toms'er gnel?]
ticket	**տոմս** [toms]
to buy a ticket	**տոմս գնել** [toms gnel]
ticket price	**տոմսի արժեքը** [t'omsi arzh'eqy]
Where to?	**Ո՞ւր:** [ur?]
To what station?	**Մինչև ո՞ր կայարան:** [minch'ev vor kayar'an?]
I need ...	**Ինձ հարկավոր է ...** [indz harkav'or e ...]
one ticket	**մեկ տոմս** [mek toms]
two tickets	**երկու տոմս** [yerk'u toms]
three tickets	**երեք տոմս** [yer'ek toms]
one-way	**մեկ ուղղությամբ** [mek ughghuty'amb]
round-trip	**վերադարձով** [veradardz'ov]
first class	**առաջին դաս** [araj'in das]
second class	**երկրորդ դաս** [yerkr'ord das]
today	**այսօր** [ays'or]
tomorrow	**վաղը** [v'aghy]
the day after tomorrow	**վաղը չէ մյուս օրը** [v'aghy che my'us 'ory]
in the morning	**առավոտյան** [aravoty'an]
in the afternoon	**ցերեկը** [tser'eky]
in the evening	**երեկոյան** [yerekoy'an]

aisle seat	**տեղ միջանցքի մոտ** [tegh mijantsk'i mot]
window seat	**տեղ պատուհանի մոտ** [tegh patuhan'i mot]
How much?	**Ինչքա՞ն:** [inchq'an?]
Can I pay by credit card?	**Կարո՞ղ եմ վճարել քարտով:** [kar'ogh am vchar'el qart'ov?]

Bus

bus	**ավտոբուս** [avtob'us]
intercity bus	**միջքաղաքային ավտոբուս** [mijqaghaqay'in avtob'us]
bus stop	**ավտոբուսի կանգառ** [avtob'usi kang'ar]
Where's the nearest bus stop?	**Որտե՞ղ է մոտակա ավտոբուսի կանգառը:** [vort'egh e motak'a avtob'usi kang'ary?]

---

number (bus ~, etc.)	**համար** [ham'ar]
Which bus do I take to get to ...?	**Ո՞ր ավտոբուսն է գնում մինչև ...:** [vor avtob'usn e gnum minch'ev ...?]
Does this bus go to ...?	**Այս ավտոբուսը գնու՞մ է մինչև ...:** [ays avtob'usy gnum e minch'ev ...?]
How frequent are the buses?	**Որքա՞ն հաճախ են երթևեկում ավտոբուսները:** [vorq'an hach'akh en gnum avtob'usnery?]

---

every 15 minutes	**յուրաքանչյուր տասնհինգ րոպեն մեկ** [yurakanchy'ur tasnh'ing rop'en mek]
every half hour	**յուրաքանչյուր կեսժամը մեկ** [yurakanchy'ur kes jam'y mek]
every hour	**յուրաքանչյուր ժամը մեկ** [yurakanchy'ur jam'y mek]
several times a day	**օրեկան մի քանի անգամ** [orek'an mi qan'i ang'am]
... times a day	**օրեկան ... անգամ** [orek'an ... ang'am]

---

schedule	**չվացուցակ** [chvatsuts'ak]
Where can I see the schedule?	**Որտե՞ղ կարելի է նայել չվացուցակը:** [vort'egh karel'i e nay'el chvatsuts'aky?]
When is the next bus?	**Ե՞րբ է լինելու հաջորդ ավտոբուսը:** [yerb e linel'u haj'ord avtob'usy?]
When is the first bus?	**Ե՞րբ է մեկնում առաջին ավտոբուսը:** [yerb e mekn'um araj'in avtob'usy?]
When is the last bus?	**Ե՞րբ է մեկնում վերջին ավտոբուսը:** [yerb e mekn'um verj'in avtob'usy?]

stop	**կանգառ** [kang'ar]
next stop	**հաջորդ կանգառ** [haj'ord kang'ar]
last stop (terminus)	**վերջին կանգառ** [verj'in kang'ar]
Stop here, please.	**Կանգնեք այստեղ, խնդրում եմ:** [kangn'ek ayst'egh, khndrum em]
Excuse me, this is my stop.	**Թույլ տվեք, սա իմ կանգառն է:** [tuyl tveq, sa im kang'arn e]

Train

train	**գնացք** [gnatsq]
suburban train	**մերձքաղաքային գնացք** [merdzqaghaqay'in gnatsq]
long-distance train	**հեռագնաց գնացք** [heragn'ac gnatsq]
train station	**կայարան** [kayar'an]
Excuse me, where is the exit to the platform?	**Ներեցեք, որտե՞ղ է ելքը դեպի գնացքները:** [nerets'eq, vort'egh e y'elky dep'i gnatsqn'ery?]
Does this train go to ...?	**Այս գնացքը գնո՞ւմ է մինչև ...:** [ays gn'atsqy gnum e minch'ev ...?]
next train	**հաջորդ գնացքը** [haj'ord gn'atsqy]
When is the next train?	**Ե՞րբ է լինելու հաջորդ գնացքը:** [yerb e linel'u haj'ord gn'atsqy?]
Where can I see the schedule?	**Որտե՞ղ կարելի է նայել չվացուցակը:** [vort'egh karel'i e nay'el chvatsuts'aky?]
From which platform?	**Ո՞ր հարթակից:** [vor hartak'its?]
When does the train arrive in ...?	**Ե՞րբ է գնացքը ժամանում ...:** [yerb e gn'atsqy zhaman'um ...?]
Please help me.	**Օգնեցեք ինձ, խնդրեմ:** [ognets'eq indz, khndrem]
I'm looking for my seat.	**Ես փնտրում եմ իմ տեղը:** [yes pntrum am im t'eghy]
We're looking for our seats.	**Մենք փնտրում ենք մեր տեղերը:** [menq pntrum enq mer tegh'ery]
My seat is taken.	**Իմ տեղը զբաղված է:** [im t'eghy zbaghv'ats e]
Our seats are taken.	**Մեր տեղերը զբաղված են:** [mer tegh'ery zbaghv'ats en]
I'm sorry but this is my seat.	**Ներեցեք, խնդրում եմ, բայց սա իմ տեղն է:** [nerets'eq, khndrum am, bayts sa im t'eghn e]

Is this seat taken?	**Այս տեղն ազա՞տ է:** [ays teghn az'at e?]
May I sit here?	**Կարո՞ղ եմ այստեղ նստել:** [kar'ogh am ayst'egh nstel?]

On the train. Dialogue (No ticket)

Ticket, please.	**Ձեր տոմսը, խնդրեմ:** [dzer t'omsy, khndrem]
I don't have a ticket.	**Ես տոմս չունեմ:** [yes toms chun'em]
I lost my ticket.	**Ես կորցրել եմ իմ տոմսը:** [yes kortsr'el am im t'omsy]
I forgot my ticket at home.	**Ես մոռացել եմ իմ տոմսը տանը:** [yes morats'el am im t'omsy t'any]
You can buy a ticket from me.	**Դուք կարող եք գնել տոմս ինձանից:** [indzan'its]
You will also have to pay a fine.	**Նաև դուք պետք է վճարեք տուգանք:** [na'ev duq petq e vchar'eq tug'ank]
Okay.	**Լավ:** [lav]
Where are you going?	**Ո՞ւր եք մեկնում:** [ur eq mekn'um?]
I'm going to ...	**Ես գնում եմ մինչև ...** [yes gnum am minch'ev ...]
How much? I don't understand.	**Ինչքա՞ն: Ես չեմ հասկանում:** [inchq'an? yes chem haskan'um]
Write it down, please.	**Գրեք, խնդրում եմ:** [grek, khndrum em]
Okay. Can I pay with a credit card?	**Լավ: Կարո՞ղ եմ վճարել քարտով:** [lav kar'ogh am vchar'el qart'ov?]
Yes, you can.	**Այո, կարող եք:** [ay'o, kar'ogh eq]
Here's your receipt.	**Ահա ձեր անդորրագիրը:** [ah'a dzer andorag'iry]
Sorry about the fine.	**Ցավում եմ տուգանքի համար:** [tsav'um am tugank'i ham'ar]
That's okay. It was my fault.	**Ոչինչ: Դա իմ մեղքն է:** [voch'inch. da im meghqn e]
Enjoy your trip.	**Հաճելի ճանապարհորդությո՛ւն:** [hachel'i chanaparhoduty'un]

Taxi

taxi	**տաքսի** [tax'i]
taxi driver	**տաքսու վարորդ** [tax'u var'ord]
to catch a taxi	**տաքսի բռնել** [tax'i brnel]
taxi stand	**տաքսու կանգառ** [tax'u kang'ar]
Where can I get a taxi?	**Որտե՞ղ կարող եմ տաքսի վերցնել:** [vort'egh kar'ogh am tax'i vertsn'el?]
to call a taxi	**տաքսի կանչել** [tax'i kanch'el]
I need a taxi.	**Ինձ տաքսի է հարկավոր:** [indz tax'i e harkav'or]
Right now.	**Հենց հիմա:** [hents him'a]
What is your address (location)?	**Ձեր հասցե՞ն:** [dzer hasc'en?]
My address is ...	**Իմ հասցեն ...** [im hasc'en ...]
Your destination?	**Ո՞ւր եք գնալու:** [ur eq gnal'u?]
Excuse me, ...	**Ներեցեք, ...** [nerets'eq, ...]
Are you available?	**Ազա՞տ եք:** [az'at eq?]
How much is it to get to ...?	**Ի՞նչ արժե հասնել մինչև ...:** [inch arzh'e hasn'el minch'ev ...?]
Do you know where it is?	**Դուք գիտե՞ք` որտեղ է դա:** [duq git'eq vort'egh e da?]
Airport, please.	**Օդանավակայան, խնդրում եմ:** [odanavakay'an, khndrum em]
Stop here, please.	**Կանգնեցրեք այստեղ, խնդրում եմ:** [kangnetsr'eq ayst'egh, khndrum em]
It's not here.	**Դա այստեղ չէ:** [da ayst'egh che]
This is the wrong address.	**Դա սխալ հասցե է:** [da skhal hasc'e e]
Turn left.	**դեպի ձախ** [dep'i dzakh]
Turn right.	**դեպի աջ** [dep'i aj]

How much do I owe you?	**Որքա՞ն պետք է վճարեմ:** [vorq'an petq e vchar'em?]
I'd like a receipt, please.	**Տվեք ինձ չեքը, խնդրում եմ:** [tveq indz ch'eqy, khndrum em]
Keep the change.	**Մանրը պետք չէ:** [m'anry petq che]

Would you please wait for me?	**Սպասեք ինձ, խնդրում եմ:** [spas'eq indz, khndrum em]
five minutes	**հինգ րոպե** [hing rop'e]
ten minutes	**տաս րոպե** [tas rop'e]
fifteen minutes	**տասնհինգ րոպե** [tasnh'ing rop'e]
twenty minutes	**քսան րոպե** [qsan rop'e]
half an hour	**կես ժամ** [kes zham]

Hotel

Hello.
Բարև Ձեզ:
[bar'ev dzez]

My name is …
Իմ անունը … է:
[im an'uny … e]

I have a reservation.
Ես համար եմ ամրագրել:
[yes ham'ar am amragr'el]

I need …
Ինձ հարկավոր է …
[indz harkav'or e …]

a single room
մեկտեղանոց համար
[mekteghan'ots ham'ar]

a double room
երկտեղանոց համար
[yerkteghan'ots ham'ar]

How much is that?
Որքա՞ն այն արժե:
[vorq'an ayn arzh'e?]

That's a bit expensive.
Դա մի քիչ թանկ է:
[da mi qich tank e]

Do you have any other options?
Ունե՞ք որևէ այլ տարբերակ:
[un'eq vorev'e 'ayl tarber'ak?]

I'll take it.
Ես դա կվերցնեմ:
[yes da kvertsn'em]

I'll pay in cash.
Ես կանխիկ կվճարեմ:
[yes kankh'ik kvchar'em]

I've got a problem.
Ես խնդիր ունեմ:
[yes khnd'ir un'em]

My … is broken.
Իմ … փչացել է:
[im … pchats'el e]

My … is out of order.
Իմ … չի աշխատում:
[im … chi ashkhat'um]

TV
հեռուստացույցը
[herustats'uytsy]

air conditioning
օդորակիչը
[odorak'ichy]

tap
ծորակը
[tsor'aky]

---

shower
ցնցուղը
[tsnts'ughy]

sink
լվացարանը
[lvatsar'any]

safe
չհրկիզվող պահարանը
[chhrkizv'ogh pahar'any]

door lock	**կողպեքը** [koghp'eqy]
electrical outlet	**վարդակը** [vard'aky]
hairdryer	**ֆենը** [f'eny]

I don't have ...	**Ես ... չունեմ:** [yes ... chun'em]
water	**ջուր** [jur]
light	**լույս** [luys]
electricity	**հոսանք** [hos'anq]

Can you give me ...?	**Կարո՞ղ եք ինձ տալ ...:** [kar'ogh eq indz tal ...?]
a towel	**սրբիչ** [srbich]
a blanket	**ծածկոց** [tsatsk'ots]
slippers	**հողաթափեր** [hoghatap'er]
a robe	**խալաթ** [khal'at]
shampoo	**շամպուն** [shamp'un]
soap	**օճառ** [och'ar]

I'd like to change rooms.	**Ես կցանկանայի փոխել համարս:** [yes ktsankan'ayi pokh'el ham'ars]
I can't find my key.	**Ես չեմ կարողանում գտնել իմ բանալին:** [yes chem karoghan'um gtnel im banal'in]
Could you open my room, please?	**Խնդրում եմ, բացեք իմ համարը:** [khndrum em, bats'ek im ham'ary]
Who's there?	**Ո՞վ է:** [ov e?]
Come in!	**Մտեք:** [mteq!]
Just a minute!	**Մեկ րոպե:** [mek rope!]
Not right now, please.	**Խնդրում եմ, հիմա չէ:** [khndrum em, him'a che]

Come to my room, please.	**Խնդրում եմ, ինձ մոտ մտեք:** [khndrum em, indz mot mteq]
I'd like to order food service.	**Ես ուզում եմ ուտելիք համար պատվիրել:** [yes uz'um am utel'iq ham'ar patvir'el]

My room number is ...	**Իմ սենյակի համարը ... է:** [im senyak'i ham'ary ... e]
I'm leaving ...	**Ես մեկնում եմ ...** [yes mekn'um am ...]
We're leaving ...	**Մենք մեկնում ենք ...** [menq mekn'um enq ...]
right now	**հիմա** [him'a]
this afternoon	**այսօր ճաշից հետո** [ays'or chash'its het'o]
tonight	**այսօր երեկոյան** [ays'or yerekoy'an]
tomorrow	**վաղը** [v'aghy]
tomorrow morning	**վաղն առավոտյան** [v'aghn aravoty'an]
tomorrow evening	**վաղը երեկոյան** [v'aghy yerekoy'an]
the day after tomorrow	**վաղը չէ մյուս օրը** [v'aghy che my'us 'ory]

I'd like to pay.	**Ես կուզենայի հաշիվը փակել:** [yes kuzen'ayi hash'ivy pak'el]
Everything was wonderful.	**Ամեն ինչ հոյակապ էր:** [am'en inch hoyak'ap er]
Where can I get a taxi?	**Որտե՞ղ կարող եմ տաքսի վերցնել:** [vort'egh kar'ogh am tax'i vertsn'el?]
Would you call a taxi for me, please?	**Ինձ համար տաքսի կանչեք, խնդրում եմ:** [indz ham'ar tax'i kanch'eq, khndrum em]

Restaurant

Can I look at the menu, please?	**Կարո՞ղ եմ նայել ձեր ճաշացանկը:** [kar'ogh am nay'el dzer chashats'anky?]
Table for one.	**Սեղան մեկ հոգու համար:** [segh'an mek hog'u ham'ar]
There are two (three, four) of us.	**Մենք երկուսով (երեքով, չորսով) ենք:** [menq yerkus'ov (yerek'ov, chors'ov) enq]
Smoking	**Ծխողների համար** [tskhoghner'i ham'ar]
No smoking	**Չծխողների համար** [chtskhoghner'i ham'ar]
Excuse me! (addressing a waiter)	**Մոտեցեք խնդրեմ:** [motets'eq khndrem!]
menu	**Ճաշացանկ** [chashats'ank]
wine list	**Գինեքարտ** [gineq'art]
The menu, please.	**Ճաշացանկը, խնդրեմ:** [chashats'anky, khndrem]
Are you ready to order?	**Պատրա՞ստ եք պատվիրել:** [patr'ast eq patvir'el?]
What will you have?	**Ի՞նչ եք պատվիրելու:** [inch eq patvirel'u?]
I'll have ...	**Ես կվերցնեմ ...** [yes kvertsn'em ...]
I'm a vegetarian.	**Ես բուսակեր եմ:** [yes busak'er am]
meat	**միս** [mis]
fish	**ձուկ** [dzuk]
vegetables	**բանջարեղեն** [banjaregh'en]
Do you have vegetarian dishes?	**Դուք ունե՞ք բուսակերական ճաշատեսակներ:** [duq un'eq busakerak'an chashatesakn'er?]
I don't eat pork.	**Ես խոզի միս չեմ ուտում:** [yes kh'ozi mis chem ut'um]
He /she/ doesn't eat meat.	**Նա միս չի ուտում:** [na mis chi ut'um]

I am allergic to ...	**Ես ...ից ալերգիա ունեմ:** [yes ...its alerg'ia un'em]
Would you please bring me ...	**Խնդրում եմ, ինձ ... բերեք:** [khndrum em, indz ... ber'eq]
salt | pepper | sugar	**աղ | պղպեղ | շաքար** [agh | pghpegh | shaq'ar]
coffee | tea | dessert	**սուրճ | թեյ | աղանդեր** [surch | tey | aghand'er]
water | sparkling | plain	**ջուր | գազավորված | չգազավորված** [jur | gazavorv'ats | chgazavorv'ats]
a spoon | fork | knife	**գդալ | պատառաքաղ | դանակ** [gdal | pataraq'agh | dan'ak]
a plate | napkin	**ափսե | անձեռոցիկ** [aps'e | andzerots'ik]

Enjoy your meal!	**Բարի ախորժա՛կ:** [bar'i akhorzh'ak!]
One more, please.	**Էլի բերեք, խնդրում եմ:** [el'i ber'eq, khndrum em]
It was very delicious.	**Շատ համեղ էր:** [shat ham'egh er]

---

check | change | tip	**հաշիվ | մանրադրամ | թեյավճար** [hash'iv | manradr'am | tyeyavch'ar]
Check, please. (Could I have the check, please?)	**Հաշիվը, խնդրում եմ:** [hash'ivy, khndrum em]
Can I pay by credit card?	**Կարո՞ղ եմ վճարել քարտով:** [kar'ogh am vchar'el qart'ov?]
I'm sorry, there's a mistake here.	**Ներեցեք, այստեղ սխալ կա:** [nerets'eq, ayst'egh skhal ka]

Shopping

Can I help you?	**Կարո՞ղ եմ օգնել ձեզ:** [kar'ogh am ogn'el dzez?]
Do you have ...?	**Դուք ունե՞ք ...:** [duq un'eq ...?]
I'm looking for ...	**Ես փնտրում եմ ...** [yes pntrum am ...]
I need ...	**Ինձ պետք է ...** [indz petq e ...]
I'm just looking.	**Ես ուղղակի նայում եմ:** [yes ughghak'i nay'um am]
We're just looking.	**Մենք ուղղակի նայում ենք:** [menq ughgh'aki nay'um enq]
I'll come back later.	**Ես ավելի ուշ կայցելեմ:** [yes avel'i ush kaytsel'em]
We'll come back later.	**Մենք ավելի ուշ կայցելենք:** [menq avel'i ush kaytsel'enq]
discounts | sale	**զեղչեր | իսպառ վաճառք** [zeghch'er | isp'ar vach'arq]
Would you please show me ...	**Ցույց տվեք ինձ, խնդրում եմ ...** [tsuyts tveq indz, khndrum em ...]
Would you please give me ...	**Տվեք ինձ, խնդրում եմ ...** [tveq indz, khndrum em ...]
Can I try it on?	**Կարո՞ղ եմ ես սա փորձել:** [kar'ogh am yes sa pordz'el?]
Excuse me, where's the fitting room?	**Ներեցեք, որտե՞ղ է հանդերձարանը:** [nerets'eq, vort'egh e handerdzar'any?]
Which color would you like?	**Ի՞նչ գույն եք ուզում:** [inch guyn eq uz'um?]
size | length	**չափս | հասակ** [chaps | hasak]
How does it fit?	**Եղա՞վ:** [yegh'av?]
How much is it?	**Սա ինչքա՞ն արժե:** [sa inchq'an arzh'e?]
That's too expensive.	**Դա չափազանց թանկ է:** [da chapaz'ants tank e]
I'll take it.	**Ես կվերցնեմ սա:** [yes kvertsn'em sa]
Excuse me, where do I pay?	**Ներեցեք, որտե՞ղ է դրամարկղը:** [nerets'eq, vort'egh e dram'arkghy?]

Will you pay in cash or credit card?	**Ինչպե՞ս եք վճարելու: Կանխի՞կ թե քարտով:** [inchp'es eq vcharel'u? kankh'ik te qart'ov?]
In cash | with credit card	**կանխիկ | քարտով** [kankh'ik | qart'ov]
Do you want the receipt?	**Ձեզ չեքն անհրաժե՞շտ է:** [dzez cheqn anhrazh'esht e?]
Yes, please.	**Այո, խնդրում եմ:** [ay'o, khndrum em]
No, it's OK.	**Ոչ, պետք չէ: Շնորհակալություն:** [voch, petq che. shnorhakaluty'un]
Thank you. Have a nice day!	**Շնորհակալություն: Ցտեսություն:** [shnorhakaluty'un tstesuty'un!]

In town

Excuse me, please.	**Ներեցեք խնդրեմ ...** [nerets'eq khndrem ...]
I'm looking for ...	**Ես փնտրում եմ ...** [yes pntrum am ...]
the subway	**մետրո** [metr'o]
my hotel	**իմ հյուրանոցը** [im hyuran'otsy]
the movie theater	**կինոթատրոն** [kinotatr'on]
a taxi stand	**տաքսիների կայան** [taxiner'i kay'an]
an ATM	**բանկոմատ** [bankom'at]
a foreign exchange office	**արժույթի փոխանակման կետ** [arzhuyt'i pvokhanakm'an ket]
an internet café	**ինտերնետ-սրճարան** [intern'et-srchar'an]
... street	**... փողոցը** [... pogh'otsy]
this place	**այս տեղը** ['ays t'eghy]
Do you know where ... is?	**Դուք գիտե՞ք՝ որտեղ է գտնվում ...:** [duq git'eq vort'egh e gtnv'um ...?]
Which street is this?	**Ինչպե՞ս է կոչվում այս փողոցը:** [inchp'es e kochv'um ays pvogh'otsy?]
Show me where we are right now.	**Ցույց տվեք՝ որտեղ ենք մենք հիմա:** [tsuyts tveq vort'egh enq menq him'a]
Can I get there on foot?	**Ես կհասնե՞մ այնտեղ ոտքով:** [yes khasn'em aynt'egh votq'ov?]
Do you have a map of the city?	**Դուք ունե՞ք քաղաքի քարտեզը:** [duq un'eq qagh'aqi qart'ezy?]
How much is a ticket to get in?	**Որքա՞ն արժե մուտքի տոմսը:** [vorq'an arzh'e mutqi t'omsy?]
Can I take pictures here?	**Այստեղ կարելի՞ է լուսանկարել:** [ayst'egh karel'i e lusankar'el?]
Are you open?	**Դուք բա՞ց եք:** [duq b'ats eq?]

When do you open?	**Ժամը քանիսի՞ն եք դուք բացվում:** [zh'amy qanis'in eq duq batsv'um?]
When do you close?	**Մինչև ո՞ր ժամն եք աշխատում:** [minch'ev vor zhamn eq ashkhat'um?]

Money

money	փող [pogh]
cash	կանխիկ դրամ [kankh'ik dram]
paper money	թղթադրամ [tghtadr'am]
loose change	մանրադրամ [manradr'am]
check | change | tip	հաշիվ | մանր | թեյավճար [hash'iv | manr | tyeyavch'ar]
credit card	կրեդիտ քարտ [kred'it qart]
wallet	դրամապանակ [dramapan'ak]
to buy	գնել [gnel]
to pay	վճարել [vchar'el]
fine	տուգանք [tug'anq]
free	անվճար [anvch'ar]
Where can I buy …?	Որտե՞ղ կարող եմ գնել …: [vort'egh kar'ogh am gnel …?]
Is the bank open now?	Բանկը հիմա բա՞ց է: [b'anky him'a bats e?]
When does it open?	Ժամը քանիսի՞ն է այն բացվում: [zh'amy qanis'in e 'ayn batsv'um?]
When does it close?	Մինչև ո՞ր ժամն է այն աշխատում: [minch'ev vor zhamn e 'ayn ashkhat'um?]
How much?	Ինչքա՞ն: [inchq'an?]
How much is this?	Սա ինչքա՞ն արժե: [sa inchq'an arzh'e?]
That's too expensive.	Դա չափազանց թանկ է: [da chapaz'ants tank e]
Excuse me, where do I pay?	Ներեցեք, որտե՞ղ է դրամարկղը: [nerets'eq, vort'egh e dram'arkghy?]
Check, please.	Հաշիվը, խնդրում եմ: [hash'ivy, khndrum em]

Can I pay by credit card?	**Կարո՞ղ եմ վճարել քարտով:** [kar'ogh am vchar'el qart'ov?]
Is there an ATM here?	**Այստեղ բանկոմատ կա՞:** [ayst'egh bankom'at ka?]
I'm looking for an ATM.	**Ինձ բանկոմատ է հարկավոր:** [indz bankom'at e harkav'or?]

I'm looking for a foreign exchange office.	**Ես փնտրում եմ փոխանակման կետ:** [yes pntrum am pokhanakm'an ket]
I'd like to change ...	**Ես ուզում եմ փոխանակել ...** [yes uz'um am pokhanak'el ...]
What is the exchange rate?	**Ասացեք, խնդրեմ, փոխարժեքը:** [asats'eq, khndrem, pokharzh'eqy?]
Do you need my passport?	**Ձեզ պե՞տք է իմ անձնագիրը:** [dzez petq e im andznag'iry?]

Time

What time is it?	**Ժամը քանի՞սն է:** [zh'amy qan'isn e?]
When?	**Ե՞րբ:** [yerb?]
At what time?	**Ժամը քանիսի՞ն:** [zh'amy qanis'in?]
now | later | after ...	**հիմա | ավելի ուշ | ...ից հետո** [him'a | avel'i ush | ...its het'o]
one o'clock	**ցերեկվա ժամը մեկը** [tserekv'a zh'amy m'eky]
one fifteen	**մեկն անց տասնհինգ րոպե** [mekn ants tasnh'ing rop'e]
one thirty	**մեկն անց կես** [m'ekn ants kes]
one forty-five	**երկուսին տասնհինգ պակաս** [yerkus'in tasnh'ing pak'as]
one | two | three	**մեկ | երկու | երեք** [mek | yerk'u | yer'ek]
four | five | six	**չորս | հինգ | վեց** [chors | hing | vets]
seven | eight | nine	**յոթ | ութ | ինը** [yot | ut | 'iny]
ten | eleven | twelve	**տաս | տասնմեկ | տասներկու** [tas | tasnm'ek | tasnerk'u]
in ...	**...ից** [...its]
five minutes	**հինգ րոպե** [hing rop'e]
ten minutes	**տաս րոպե** [tas rop'e]
fifteen minutes	**տասնհինգ րոպե** [tasnh'ing rop'e]
twenty minutes	**քսան րոպե** [qsan rop'e]
half an hour	**կես ժամ** [kes zham]
an hour	**մեկ ժամ** [mek zham]

in the morning	**առավոտյան** [aravoty'an]
early in the morning	**վաղ առավոտյան** [vagh aravoty'an]
this morning	**այսօր առավոտյան** [ays'or aravoty'an]
tomorrow morning	**վաղն առավոտյան** [v'aghn aravoty'an]
at noon	**ճաշին** [chash'in]
in the afternoon	**ճաշից հետո** [chash'its het'o]
in the evening	**երեկոյան** [yerekoy'an]
tonight	**այսօր երեկոյան** [ays'or yerekoy'an]
at night	**գիշերը** [gish'ery]
yesterday	**երեկ** [yer'ek]
today	**այսօր** [ays'or]
tomorrow	**վաղը** [v'aghy]
the day after tomorrow	**վաղը չէ մյուս օրը** [v'aghy che my'us 'ory]
What day is it today?	**Շաբաթվա ի՞նչ օր է այսօր:** [shabatv'a inch or e ays'or?]
It's ...	**Այսօր ... է:** [ays'or ... e]
Monday	**երկուշաբթի** [yerkushabt'i]
Tuesday	**երեքշաբթի** [yerekshabt'i]
Wednesday	**չորեքշաբթի** [choreqshabt'i]
Thursday	**հինգշաբթի** [hingshabt'i]
Friday	**ուրբաթ** [urb'at]
Saturday	**շաբաթ** [shab'at]
Sunday	**կիրակի** [kirak'i]

Greetings. Introductions

Hello.	**Բարև Ձեզ։** [bar'ev dzez]
Pleased to meet you.	**Ուրախ եմ ձեզ հետ ծանոթանալու։** [ur'akh am dzez het tsanotanal'u]
Me too.	**Նմանապես։** [nmanap'es]
I'd like you to meet ...	**Ծանոթացեք։ Սա ... է։** [tsanotats'ek. sa ... e]
Nice to meet you.	**Շատ հաճելի է։** [shat hachel'i e]
How are you?	**Ինչպե՞ս եք։ Ինչպե՞ս են ձեր գործերը։** [inchp'es eq? inchp'es en dzer gorts'ery?]
My name is ...	**Իմ անունը ... է։** [im an'uny ... e]
His name is ...	**Նրա անունը ... է։** [nra an'uny ... e]
Her name is ...	**Նրա անունը ... է։** [nra an'uny ... e]
What's your name?	**Ձեր անունն ի՞նչ է։** [dzer an'unn inch e?]
What's his name?	**Ի՞նչ է նրա անունը։** [inch e nra an'uny?]
What's her name?	**Ի՞նչ է նրա անունը։** [inch e nra an'uny?]
What's your last name?	**Ի՞նչ է ձեր ազգանունը։** [inch e dzer azgan'uny?]
You can call me ...	**Ասացեք ինձ ...** [asac'eq indz ...]
Where are you from?	**Որտեղի՞ց եք դուք։** [vortegh'its eq duq?]
I'm from ...	**Ես ...ից եմ։** [yes ...its am]
What do you do for a living?	**Որտե՞ղ եք աշխատում։** [vort'egh eq ashkhat'um?]
Who is this?	**Ո՞վ է սա։** [ov e sa?]
Who is he?	**Ո՞վ է նա։** [ov e na?]
Who is she?	**Ո՞վ է նա։** [ov e na?]
Who are they?	**Ո՞վ են նրանք։** [ov en nr'ank?]

This is ...	**Սա ...ն է:** [sa ...n e]
my friend (masc.)	**իմ ընկեր** [im ynk'er]
my friend (fem.)	**իմ ընկերուհի** [im ynkeruh'i]
my husband	**իմ ամուսին** [im amus'in]
my wife	**իմ կին** [im kin]
my father	**իմ հայր** [im hayr]
my mother	**իմ մայր** [im mayr]
my brother	**իմ եղբայր** [im yeghb'ayr]
my sister	**իմ քույր** [im quyr]
my son	**իմ որդի** [im vord'i]
my daughter	**իմ դուստր** [im dustr]
This is our son.	**Սա մեր որդին է:** [sa mer vord'in e]
This is our daughter.	**Սա մեր դուստրն է:** [sa mer d'ustrn e]
These are my children.	**Սրանք իմ երեխաներն են:** [srank im yerekhan'ern en]
These are our children.	**Սրանք մեր երեխաներն են:** [srank mer yerekhan'ern en]

Farewells

Good bye!	**Ցտեսություն։** [tstesuty'un!]
Bye! (inform.)	**Հաջող։** [haj'ogh!]
See you tomorrow.	**Մինչ վաղը։** [minch v'aghy]
See you soon.	**Մինչ հանդիպում։** [minch handip'um]
See you at seven.	**Կհանդիպենք ժամը յոթին։** [khandip'enk zh'amy yot'in]
Have fun!	**Զվարճացեք։** [zvarchats'eq!]
Talk to you later.	**Հետո կխոսենք։** [het'o kkhos'enq]
Have a nice weekend.	**Հաջող հանգստյան օրեր եմ ցանկանում։** [haj'ogh hangsty'an or'er am tsankan'um]
Good night.	**Բարի գիշեր։** [bar'i gish'er]
It's time for me to go.	**Գնալուս ժամանակն է։** [gnal'us zhaman'akn e]
I have to go.	**Ես պետք է գնամ։** [yes petq e gnam]
I will be right back.	**Ես հիմա կվերադառնամ։** [yes him'a kveradarn'am]
It's late.	**Արդեն ուշ է։** [ard'en 'ush e]
I have to get up early.	**Ես պետք է վաղ արթնանամ։** [yes petq e vagh artnan'am]
I'm leaving tomorrow.	**Ես վաղը մեկնում եմ։** [yes v'aghy mekn'um am]
We're leaving tomorrow.	**Մենք վաղը մեկնում ենք։** [menq v'aghy mekn'um enq]
Have a nice trip!	**Բարի ճանապա˜րհ։** [bar'i chanap'arh!]
It was nice meeting you.	**Հաճելի էր ձեզ հետ ծանոթանալ։** [hachel'i er dzez het tsanotan'al]
It was nice talking to you.	**Հաճելի էր ձեզ հետ շփվել։** [hachel'i er dzez het shpv'el]
Thanks for everything.	**Շնորհակալություն ամեն ինչի համար։** [shnorhakaluty'un am'en inch'i ham'ar]

I had a very good time.	**Ես հոյակապ անցկացրեցի ժամանակը:** [yes hoyak'ap antskatsrets'i zhaman'aky]
We had a very good time.	**Մենք հոյակապ անցկացրեցինք ժամանակը:** [menq hoyak'ap antskatsrets'inq zhaman'aky]
It was really great.	**Ամեն ինչ հոյակապ էր:** [am'en inch hoyak'ap er]
I'm going to miss you.	**Ես կկարոտեմ:** [yes kkarot'em]
We're going to miss you.	**Մենք կկարոտենք:** [menq kkarot'enq]

Good luck!	**Հաջողությո˜ւն: Մնաք բարո˜վ:** [hajoghuty'un! mnaq baro'v!]
Say hi to ...	**Բարևեք ...ին:** [barev'eq ...in]

Foreign language

I don't understand. — **Ես չեմ հասկանում:**
[yes chem haskan'um]

Write it down, please. — **Խնդրում եմ, գրեք դա:**
[khndrum em, greq da]

Do you speak ...? — **Դուք գիտե՞ք ...:**
[duq git'eq ...?]

I speak a little bit of ... — **Ես գիտեմ մի քիչ ...**
[yes git'em mi qich ...]

English — **անգլերեն**
[angler'en]

Turkish — **թուրքերեն**
[turker'en]

Arabic — **արաբերեն**
[araber'en]

French — **ֆրանսերեն**
[franser'en]

German — **գերմաներեն**
[germaner'en]

Italian — **իտալերեն**
[italer'en]

Spanish — **իսպաներեն**
[ispaner'en]

Portuguese — **պորտուգալերեն**
[portugaler'en]

Chinese — **չիներեն**
[chiner'en]

Japanese — **ճապոներեն**
[chaponer'en]

Can you repeat that, please. — **Կրկնեք, խնդրեմ:**
[krkneq, khndrem]

I understand. — **Ես հասկանում եմ:**
[yes haskan'um am]

I don't understand. — **Ես չեմ հասկանում:**
[yes chem haskan'um]

Please speak more slowly. — **Խոսեք դանդաղ, խնդրում եմ:**
[khos'eq dand'agh, khndrum em]

Is that correct? (Am I saying it right?) — **Սա ճ՞իշտ է:**
[sa chisht e?]

What is this? (What does this mean?) — **Ի՞նչ է սա:**
[inch e sa?]

Apologies

Excuse me, please.	**Ներեցեք, խնդրեմ:** [nerets'eq, khndrem]
I'm sorry.	**Ցավում եմ:** [tsav'um am]
I'm really sorry.	**Շատ ափսոս:** [shat aps'os]
Sorry, it's my fault.	**Իմ մեղավորությունն է:** [im meghavoruty'unn e]
My mistake.	**Իմ սխալն է:** [im skh'aln e]
May I ...?	**Ես կարո՞ղ եմ ...:** [yes kar'ogh am ...?]
Do you mind if I ...?	**Դեմ չե՞ք լինի, եթե ես ...:** [dem cheq lini, yet'e yes ...?]
It's OK.	**Սարսափելի ոչինչ չկա:** [sarsap'eli voch'inch chka]
It's all right.	**Ամեն ինչ կարգին է:** [am'en inch karg'in e]
Don't worry about it.	**Մի անհանգստացեք:** [mi anhangstats'eq]

Agreement

Yes.	**Այո:** [ay'o]
Yes, sure.	**Այո, իհարկե:** [ay'o, ih'arke]
OK (Good!)	**Լա՜վ:** [lav!]
Very well.	**Շատ լավ:** [shat lav]
Certainly!	**Իհարկե:** [ih'arke]
I agree.	**Ես համաձայն եմ:** [yes hamadz'ayn am]

That's correct.	**Ճիշտ է:** [chisht e]
That's right.	**Ճիշտ է:** [chisht e]
You're right.	**Դուք իրավացի եք:** [duq iravats'i eq]
I don't mind.	**Ես չեմ առարկում:** [yes chem arark'um]
Absolutely right.	**Բացարձակ ճիշտ է:** [batsardz'ak ch'isht e]

It's possible.	**Հնարավոր է:** [hnarav'or e]
That's a good idea.	**Լավ միտք է:** [lav mitq e]
I can't say no.	**Չեմ կարող մերժել:** [chem kar'ogh merzh'el]
I'd be happy to.	**Ուրախ կլինեմ:** [ur'akh klin'em]
With pleasure.	**Հաճույքով:** [hachuyq'ov]

Refusal. Expressing doubt

No.	**Ոչ:** [voch]
Certainly not.	**Իհարկե, ոչ:** [ih'arke, voch]
I don't agree.	**Ես համաձայն չեմ:** [yes hamadz'ayn chem]
I don't think so.	**Ես այդպես չեմ կարծում:** [yes ayes chem karts'um]
It's not true.	**Սուտ է:** [sut e]
You are wrong.	**Դուք իրավացի չեք:** [duq iravats'i cheq]
I think you are wrong.	**Կարծում եմ՝ իրավացի չեք:** [karts'um am iravats'i cheq]
I'm not sure.	**Համոզված չեմ:** [hamozv'ats chem]
It's impossible.	**Անհնար է:** [anhn'ar e]
Nothing of the kind (sort)!	**Ո՛չ մի նման բան:** [voch mi nman ban]
The exact opposite.	**Հակառակը:** [hakar'aky!]
I'm against it.	**Ես դեմ եմ:** [yes dem am]
I don't care.	**Ինձ միևնույն է:** [indz mievn'uyn e]
I have no idea.	**Գաղափար չունեմ:** [gaghap'ar chun'em]
I doubt that.	**Կասկածում եմ, որ այդպես է:** [kaskats'um am, vor aydp'es e]
Sorry, I can't.	**Ներեցեք, չեմ կարող:** [nerets'eq, chem kar'ogh]
Sorry, I don't want to.	**Ներեցեք, չեմ ուզում:** [nerets'eq, chem uz'um]
Thank you, but I don't need this.	**Շնորհակալություն, ինձ պետք չէ:** [shnorhakaluty'un, indz petq che]
It's late.	**Արդեն ուշ է:** [ard'en 'ush e]

I have to get up early.	**Ես պետք է վաղ արթնանամ:** [yes petq e vagh artnan'am]
I don't feel well.	**Ես ինձ վատ եմ զգում:** [indz vat am zgum]

Expressing gratitude

Thank you.	**Շնորհակալություն:** [shnorhakaluty'un]
Thank you very much.	**Շատ շնորհակալ եմ:** [shat shnorhak'al am]
I really appreciate it.	**Շատ շնորհակալ եմ:** [shat shnorhak'al am]
I'm really grateful to you.	**Շնորհակալ եմ:** [shnorhak'al am]
We are really grateful to you.	**Շնորհակալ ենք:** [shnorhak'al enq]
Thank you for your time.	**Շնորհակալություն, որ ծախսեցիք ձեր ժամանակը:** [shnorhakaluty'un, vor tsakhsets'ik dzer zhaman'aky]
Thanks for everything.	**Շնորհակալություն ամեն ինչի համար:** [shnorhakaluty'un am'en inch'i ham'ar]
Thank you for ...	**Շնորհակալություն ... համար:** [shnorhakaluty'un ... ham'ar]
your help	**ձեր օգնության** [dzer ognuty'an]
a nice time	**լավ ժամանցի** [lav zhamants'i]
a wonderful meal	**հոյակապ ուտեստների** [hoyak'ap utestner'i]
a pleasant evening	**հաճելի երեկոյի** [hachel'I erekoy'i]
a wonderful day	**հիանալի օրվա** [hianal'i orv'a]
an amazing journey	**հետաքրքիր էքսկուրսիայի** [hetaqrq'ir eqskursiay'i]
Don't mention it.	**Չարժե:** [charzh'e]
You are welcome.	**Չարժե:** [charzh'e]
Any time.	**Միշտ խնդրեմ:** [misht khndrem]
My pleasure.	**Ուրախ էի օգնելու:** [ur'akh ei ognel'u]

Forget it. It's alright.	**Մոռացեք:** [morats'eq]
Don't worry about it.	**Մի անհանգստացեք:** [mi anhangstats'eq]

Congratulations. Best wishes

Congratulations!	**Շնորհավորում եմ:** [shnorhavor'um am!]
Happy birthday!	**Շնորհավոր ծննդյան օրը:** [shnorhav'or tsnndy'an 'ory!]
Merry Christmas!	**Շնորհավոր Սուրբ ծնունդ:** [shnorhav'or surb tsnund!]
Happy New Year!	**Շնորհավոր Ամանոր:** [shnorhav'or aman'or!]
Happy Easter!	**Շնորհավոր Զատիկ:** [shnorhav'or zat'ik!]
Happy Hanukkah!	**Ուրախ Հանուկա:** [ur'akh h'anuka!]
I'd like to propose a toast.	**Ես կենաց ունեմ:** [yes ken'ats un'em]
Cheers!	**Ձեր առողջության կենացը:** [dzer aroghjuty'an ken'atsy!]
Let's drink to ...!	**Խմե՛նք ... համար:** [khmenq ... ham'ar!]
To our success!	**Մեր հաջողության կենացը:** [mer hajoghuty'an ken'atsy!]
To your success!	**Ձեր հաջողության կենացը:** [dzer hajoghuty'an ken'atsy!]
Good luck!	**Հաջողություն:** [hajoghuty'un!]
Have a nice day!	**Հաճելի օր եմ ցանկանում:** [hachel'i 'or am tsankan'um!]
Have a good holiday!	**Հաճելի հանգիստ եմ ցանկանում:** [hachel'I hang'ist am tsankan'um!]
Have a safe journey!	**Բարի ճանապարհ:** [bar'i chanap'arh!]
I hope you get better soon!	**Շուտ ապաքինում եմ ցանկանում:** [shut apaqin'um am cankan'um!]

Socializing

Why are you sad?	**Ինչո՞ւ եք տխրել:** [inxh'u eq tkhrel?]
Smile! Cheer up!	**Ժպտացե՛ք:** [zhptatsy'ek!]
Are you free tonight?	**Դուք զբաղվա՞ծ եք այսօր երեկոյան:** [duq zbaghv'ats eq ays'or yerekoy'an?]
May I offer you a drink?	**Կարո՞ղ եմ առաջարկել ձեզ որևէ ըմպելիք:** [kar'ogh am arajark'el dzez vorev'e ympel'iq?]
Would you like to dance?	**Չե՞ք ցանկանա պարել:** [cheq tsankan'a par'el?]
Let's go to the movies.	**Գնա՞նք կինոթատրոն:** [gnanq kinotatr'on?]
May I invite you to ...?	**Կարո՞ղ եմ հրավիրել ձեզ ...:** [kar'ogh am hravir'el dzez ...?]
a restaurant	**ռեստորան** [rrestor'an]
the movies	**կինոթատրոն** [kinotatr'on]
the theater	**թատրոն** [tatr'on]
go for a walk	**զբոսանքի** [zbosanq'i]
At what time?	**Ժամը քանիսի՞ն:** [zh'amy qanis'in?]
tonight	**այսօր երեկոյան** [ays'or yerekoy'an]
at six	**ժամը վեցին** [zh'amy vec'in]
at seven	**ժամը յոթին** [zh'amy yot'in]
at eight	**ժամը ութին** [zh'amy out'in]
at nine	**ժամը իննին** [zh'amy inn'in]
Do you like it here?	**Ձեզ այստեղ դո՞ւր է գալիս:** [dzez ayst'egh dur e gal'is?]
Are you here with someone?	**Դուք այստեղ ինչ-որ մեկի հե՞տ եք:** [duq ayst'egh 'inch-vor mek'i het eq?]

I'm with my friend.	**Ես ընկերոջս /ընկերուհուս/ հետ եմ:** [yes ynker'ojs /ynkeruh'us/ het am]
I'm with my friends.	**Ես ընկերներիս հետ եմ:** [yes ynkerner'is het am]
No, I'm alone.	**Ես մենակ եմ:** [yes men'ak am]
Do you have a boyfriend?	**Դու ընկեր ունե՞ս:** [du ynk'er un'es?]
I have a boyfriend.	**Ես ընկեր ունեմ:** [yes ynk'er un'em]
Do you have a girlfriend?	**Դու ընկերուհի ունե՞ս:** [du ynkeruh'i un'es?]
I have a girlfriend.	**Ես ընկերուհի ունեմ:** [yes ynkeruh'i un'em]
Can I see you again?	**Մենք դեռ կհանդիպե՞նք:** [menq der khandip'enq?]
Can I call you?	**Կարո՞ղ եմ քեզ զանգահարել:** [kar'ogh am qez zangahar'el?]
Call me. (Give me a call.)	**Կզանգես:** [kzang'es]
What's your number?	**Ո՞նց է համարդ** [vonts e ham'ard?]
I miss you.	**Ես կարոտում եմ քեզ:** [yes karot'um am qez]
You have a beautiful name.	**Դուք շատ գեղեցիկ անուն ունեք:** [duq shat geghets'ik an'un un'eq]
I love you.	**Ես սիրում եմ քեզ:** [yes sir'um am qez]
Will you marry me?	**Արի՛ ամուսնանանք:** [ar'i amusnan'anq]
You're kidding!	**Դուք կատակում եք:** [duq katak'um eq!]
I'm just kidding.	**Ես ուղղակի կատակում եմ:** [yes ughghak'i katak'um am]
Are you serious?	**Դուք լո՞ւրջ եք ասում:** [duq l'urj eq as'um?]
I'm serious.	**Ես լուրջ եմ ասում:** [yes lurj am as'um]
Really?!	**Իրո՞ք:** [ir'oq?!]
It's unbelievable!	**Դա անհավանական է:** [da anhavanak'an e!]
I don't believe you.	**Ես ձեզ չեմ հավատում:** [yes dzez chem havat'um]
I can't.	**Ես չեմ կարող:** [yes chem kar'ogh]
I don't know.	**Ես չգիտեմ:** [yes chgit'em]

I don't understand you.	**Ես ձեզ չեմ հասկանում։** [yes dzez chem haskan'um]
Please go away.	**Հեռացեք, խնդրում եմ։** [herats'ek, khndrum em]
Leave me alone!	**Ինձ հանգի՛ստ թողեք։** [indz hang'ist togh'eq]

I can't stand him.	**Ես նրան տանել չեմ կարողանում։** [yes nran tan'el chem karoghan'um]
You are disgusting!	**Դուք զզվելի եք։** [duq zzvel'i eq!]
I'll call the police!	**Ես ոստիկանություն կկանչեմ։** [yes vostikanuty'un kkanch'em!]

Sharing impressions. Emotions

I like it.	**Ինձ դա դուր է գալիս:** [indz da dur e gal'is]
Very nice.	**Հաճելի է:** [hachel'i e]
That's great!	**Հրաշալի է:** [hrashal'i e!]
It's not bad.	**Վատ չէ:** [vat che]
I don't like it.	**Սա ինձ դուր է գալիս:** [indz dur e gal'is]
It's not good.	**Դա լավ չի:** [da lav chi]
It's bad.	**Դա վատ է:** [da vat e]
It's very bad.	**Դա շատ վատ է:** [da shat vat e]
It's disgusting.	**Զզվելի է:** [zzvel'i e]
I'm happy.	**Ես երջանիկ եմ:** [yes yerjan'ik am]
I'm content.	**Ես գոհ եմ:** [yes goh am]
I'm in love.	**Ես սիրահարվել եմ:** [yes siraharv'el am]
I'm calm.	**Ես հանգիստ եմ:** [yes hang'ist am]
I'm bored.	**Ես ձանձրանում եմ:** [yes dzandzran'um am]
I'm tired.	**Ես հոգնել եմ:** [yes hogn'el am]
I'm sad.	**Ես տխուր եմ:** [yes tkhur am]
I'm frightened.	**Ես վախեցած եմ:** [yes vakhets'ats am]
I'm angry.	**Ես զայրանում եմ:** [yes zayran'um am]
I'm worried.	**Ես անհանգստանում եմ:** [yes anhangstan'um am]
I'm nervous.	**Ես ջղայնանում եմ:** [yes jghaynan'um am]

I'm jealous. (envious)
Ես նախանձում եմ:
[yes nakhandz'um am]

I'm surprised.
Ես զարմացած եմ:
[yes zarmats'ats am]

I'm perplexed.
Ես շփոթված եմ:
[yes shpvotv'ats am]

Problems. Accidents

I've got a problem.	**Ես խնդիր ունեմ:** [yes khndir un'em]
We've got a problem.	**Մենք խնդիրներ ունենք:** [menq khndirn'er un'enq]
I'm lost.	**Ես մոլորվել եմ:** [yes molorv'el am]
I missed the last bus (train).	**Ես ուշացել եմ վերջին ավտոբուսից (գնացքից):** [yes ushats'el am verj'in avtob'usits (gnatsq'its)]
I don't have any money left.	**Ինձ մոտ դրամ ընդհանրապես չի մնացել:** [indz mot dram yndhanrap'es chi mnats'el]

I've lost my ...	**Ես կորցրել եմ ...** [yes kortsr'el am ...]
Someone stole my ...	**Ինձ մոտից գողացել են ...** [indz mot'its goghats'el en ...]
passport	**անձնագիրը** [andznag'iry]
wallet	**դրամապանակը** [dramapan'aky]
papers	**փաստաթղթերը** [pastatght'ery]
ticket	**տոմսը** [t'omsy]
money	**փողը** [p'oghy]
handbag	**պայուսակը** [payus'aky]
camera	**ֆոտոապարատը** [fotoapar'aty]
laptop	**նոութբուքը** [noteb'ooky]
tablet computer	**պլանշետը** [plansh'ety]
mobile phone	**հեռախոսը** [herakh'osy]

Help me!	**Օգնե՜ցե՜ք:** [ognets'eq!]
What's happened?	**Ի՞նչ է պատահել:** [inch e patah'el?]

fire	**հրդեհ** [hrdeh]
shooting	**կրակոց** [krak'ots]
murder	**սպանություն** [spanuty'un]
explosion	**պայթյուն** [payty'un]
fight	**կռիվ** [kriv]

Call the police!	**Ոստիկանություն կանչեք:** [vostikanuty'un kanch'eq!]
Please hurry up!	**Արագացրեք, խնդրում եմ:** [aragatsr'eq, khndrum em!]
I'm looking for the police station.	**Ես փնտրում եմ ոստիկանության բաժին** [yes pntrum am vostikanuty'an bazh'in]
I need to make a call.	**Ինձ պետք է զանգահարել:** [indz petq e zangahar'el]
May I use your phone?	**Կարո՞ղ եմ զանգահարել:** [kar'ogh am zangahar'el?]

I've been ...	**Ինձ ...** [indz ...]
mugged	**կողոպտել են** [koghopt'el en]
robbed	**թալանել են** [talan'el en]
raped	**բռնաբարել են** [brnabar'el en]
attacked (beaten up)	**ծեծել են** [tsets'el en]

Are you all right?	**Ձեզ հետ ամեն ինչ կարգի՞ն է:** [dzez het am'en inch karg'in e?]
Did you see who it was?	**Դուք տեսե՞լ եք, ով էր նա:** [duq tes'el eq, ov er na?]
Would you be able to recognize the person?	**Կարո՞ղ եք նրան ճանաչել:** [kar'ogh eq nran chanach'el?]
Are you sure?	**Համոզվա՞ծ եք:** [hamozv'ats eq?]

Please calm down.	**Խնդրում եմ, հանգստացեք:** [khndrum em, hangstats'eq]
Take it easy!	**Հանգիստ:** [hang'ist!]
Don't worry!	**Մի անհանգստացեք:** [mi anhangstats'eq]
Everything will be fine.	**Ամեն ինչ լավ կլինի:** [am'en inch lav klin'i]
Everything's all right.	**Ամեն ինչ կարգին է:** [am'en inch karg'in e]

Come here, please.	**Մոտեցեք, խնդրեմ։** [motets'eq, khndrem]
I have some questions for you.	**Ես ձեզ մի քանի հարց ունեմ տալու։** [yes dzez mi qan'i harts un'em tal'u]
Wait a moment, please.	**Սպասեք, խնդրեմ։** [spas'eq, khndrem]
Do you have any I.D.?	**Դուք փաստաթղթեր ունե՞ք։** [duq pastatght'er un'eq?]
Thanks. You can leave now.	**Շնորհակալություն։** **Դուք կարող եք գնալ։** [shnorhakaluty'un. duq kar'ogh eq gnal]
Hands behind your head!	**Ձեռքերը գլխի հետև՛։** [dzerk'ery glkhi het'ev!]
You're under arrest!	**Դուք ձերբակալվա՛ծ եք։** [duq dzerbakalv'ats eq!]

Health problems

Please help me.	**Օգնեցեք, խնդրում եմ:** [ognets'eq, khndrum em]
I don't feel well.	**Ես ինձ վատ եմ զգում:** [yes indz vat am zgum]
My husband doesn't feel well.	**Իմ ամուսինն իրեն վատ է զգում:** [im amus'inn ir'en vat e zgum]
My son ...	**Իմ որդին ...** [im vord'in ...]
My father ...	**Իմ հայրն ...** [im hayrn ...]
My wife doesn't feel well.	**Իմ կինն իրեն վատ է զգում:** [im kinn ir'en vat e zgum]
My daughter ...	**Իմ դուստրն ...** [im dustrn ...]
My mother ...	**Իմ մայրն ...** [im mayrn ...]
I've got a ...	**Իմ ... ցավում է:** [im ... tsav'um e]
headache	**գլուխը** [gl'ukhy]
sore throat	**կոկորդը** [kok'ordy]
stomach ache	**փորը** [p'ory]
toothache	**ատամը** [at'amy]
I feel dizzy.	**Գլուխս պտտվում է:** [glukhs pttvum e]
He has a fever.	**Նա ջերմություն ունի:** [na jermuty'un un'i]
She has a fever.	**Նա ջերմություն ունի:** [na jermuty'un un'i]
I can't breathe.	**Ես չեմ կարողանում շնչել:** [yes chem karoghan'um shnch'el]
I'm short of breath.	**Խեղդվում եմ:** [kheghdv'um am]
I am asthmatic.	**Ես ասթմահար եմ:** [yes astmah'ar am]
I am diabetic.	**Ես շաքարախտ ունեմ:** [yes shakar'akht un'em]

I can't sleep.	**Ես անքնություն ունեմ:** [yes anknuty'un un'em]
food poisoning	**սննդային թունավորում** [snnday'in tunavor'um]

It hurts here.	**Այստեղ է ցավում:** [ayst'egh e tsav'um]
Help me!	**Օգնեցե՜ք:** [ognets'eq!]
I am here!	**Ես այստեղ եմ:** [yes ayst'egh am!]
We are here!	**Մենք այստեղ ենք:** [menq ayst'egh enq!]
Get me out of here!	**Հանեք ինձ:** [khan'ek indz!]
I need a doctor.	**Ինձ բժիշկ է պետք:** [indz bzhishk e petq]
I can't move.	**Ես չեմ կարողանում շարժվել:** [yes chem karoghan'um sharzhv'el]
I can't move my legs.	**Ես չեմ զգում ոտքերս:** [yes chem zgum votq'ers]

I have a wound.	**Ես վիրավոր եմ:** [yes virav'or am]
Is it serious?	**Լո՞ւրջ:** [lurj?]
My documents are in my pocket.	**Իմ փաստաթղթերը գրպանումս են:** [im pastatght'ery grpan'ums en]
Calm down!	**Հանգստացեք:** [hangstats'eq!]
May I use your phone?	**Կարո՞ղ եմ զանգահարել:** [kar'ogh am zangahar'el?]

Call an ambulance!	**Շտապ օգնություն կանչեք:** [shtap ognuty'un kanch'eq!]
It's urgent!	**Սա շտապ է:** [sa shtap e!]
It's an emergency!	**Սա շատ շտապ է:** [sa shat shtap e!]
Please hurry up!	**Արագացրեք, խնդրում եմ:** [aragatsr'eq, khndrum em!]
Would you please call a doctor?	**Բժիշկ կանչեք, խնդրում եմ:** [bzhishk kanch'eq, khndrum em]
Where is the hospital?	**Ասացեք, որտե՞ղ է հիվանդանոցը:** [asats'eq, vort'egh e hivandan'otsy?]

How are you feeling?	**Ինչպե՞ս եք ձեզ զգում:** [inchp'es eq dzez zgum?]
Are you all right?	**Ձեզ հետ ամեն ինչ կարգի՞ն է:** [dzez het am'en inch karg'in e?]
What's happened?	**Ի՞նչ է պատահել:** [inch e patah'el?]

I feel better now.	**Ես արդեն ինձ լավ եմ զգում:** [indz lav am zgum]
It's OK.	**Ամեն ինչ կարգին է:** [am'en inch karg'in e]
It's all right.	**Ամեն ինչ լավ է:** [am'en inch l'av e]

At the pharmacy

pharmacy (drugstore)	**դեղատուն** [deghat'un]
24-hour pharmacy	**շուրջօրյա դեղատուն** [shurjory'a deghat'un]
Where is the closest pharmacy?	**Որտե՞ղ է մոտակա դեղատունը:** [vort'egh e motak'a deghat'uny?]
Is it open now?	**Այն հիմա բա՞ց է:** [ayn him'a bats e?]
At what time does it open?	**Ժամը քանիսի՞ն է այն բացվում:** [zh'amy qanis'in e 'ayn batsv'um?]
At what time does it close?	**Մինչև ո՞ր ժամն է այն աշխատում:** [minch'ev vor zhamn e 'ayn ashkhat'um?]
Is it far?	**Դա հեռո՞ւ է:** [da her'u e?]
Can I get there on foot?	**Ես կհասնե՞մ այնտեղ ոտքով:** [yes khasn'em aynt'egh votq'ov?]
Can you show me on the map?	**Ցույց տվեք ինձ քարտեզի վրա, խնդրում եմ:** [tsuyts tveq indz qartez'i vra, khndrum am]
Please give me something for ...	**Տվեք ինձ ինչ-որ բան ... համար:** [tveq indz inch-v'or ban ... ham'ar]
a headache	**գլխացավի** [glkhatsav'i]
a cough	**հազի** [haz'i]
a cold	**մրսածության** [mrsatsuty'an]
the flu	**հարբուխի** [harbukh'i]
a fever	**ջերմության** [jermuty'an]
a stomach ache	**փորացավի** [poratsav'i]
nausea	**սրտխառնոցի** [srtkharnots'i]
diarrhea	**լուծի** [luts'i]
constipation	**փորկապության** [porkaputy'an]

pain in the back	**մեջքի ցավ** [mejk'i tsav]
chest pain	**կրծքի ցավ** [krtski tsav]
side stitch	**կողացավ** [koghats'av]
abdominal pain	**փորացավ** [porats'av]

---

pill	**հաբ** [hab]
ointment, cream	**քսուք, կրեմ** [ksuk, krem]
syrup	**օշարակ** [oshar'ak]
spray	**սփրեյ** [spr'ay]
drops	**կաթիլներ** [katiln'er]

You need to go to the hospital.	**Դուք պետք է հիվանդանոց գնաք:** [duq petq e hivandan'ots gna]
health insurance	**ապահովագրություն** [apahovagruty'un]
prescription	**դեղատոմս** [deghat'oms]
insect repellant	**միջատների դեմ միջոց** [mijatner'i dem mij'ots]
Band Aid	**լեյկոսպեղանի** [leykospeghan'i]

The bare minimum

Excuse me, …	**Ներեցեք, …** [nerets'eq, …]
Hello.	**Բարև Ձեզ։** [bar'ev dzez]
Thank you.	**Շնորհակալություն։** [shnorhakaluty'un]
Good bye.	**Ցտեսություն։** [tstesuty'un]
Yes.	**Այո։** [ay'o]
No.	**Ոչ։** [voch]
I don't know.	**Ես չգիտեմ։** [yes chgit'em]
Where? | Where to? | When?	**Ո՞րտեղ։ Ո՞ւր։ Ե՞րբ։** [vort'egh? ur? yerb?]
I need …	**Ինձ հարկավոր է …** [indz harkav'or e …]
I want …	**Ես ուզում եմ …** [yes uz'um em …]
Do you have …?	**Դուք ունե՞ք …։** [duq un'eq …?]
Is there a … here?	**Այստեղ կա՞ …։** [ayst'egh ka …?]
May I …?	**Ես կարո՞ղ եմ …։** [yes kar'ogh em …?]
…, please (polite request)	**Խնդրում եմ** [khndrum em]
I'm looking for …	**Ես փնտրում եմ …** [yes pntrum am …]
restroom	**զուգարան** [zugar'an]
ATM	**բանկոմատ** [bankom'at]
pharmacy (drugstore)	**դեղատուն** [deghat'un]
hospital	**հիվանդանոց** [hivandan'ots]
police station	**ոստիկանության բաժանմունք** [vostikanuty'an bazhanm'unq]
subway	**մետրո** [metr'o]

taxi	**տաքսի** [tax'i]
train station	**կայարան** [kayar'an]

My name is …	**Իմ անունը … է:** [im an'uny … e]
What's your name?	**Ձեր անունն ի՞նչ է:** [dzer an'unn inch e?]
Could you please help me?	**Օգնեցեք ինձ, խնդրեմ:** [ognets'eq indz, khndrem]
I've got a problem.	**Ես խնդիր ունեմ:** [yes khndir un'em]
I don't feel well.	**Ես ինձ վատ եմ զգում:** [yes indz vat am zgum]
Call an ambulance!	**Շտապ օգնություն կանչեք:** [shtap ognuty'un kanch'eq!]
May I make a call?	**Կարո՞ղ եմ զանգահարել:** [kar'ogh am zangahar'el?]

I'm sorry.	**Ներեցեք** [nerets'eq]
You're welcome.	**Խնդրեմ** [kndrem]

I, me	**ես** [yes]
you (inform.)	**դու** [du]
he	**նա** [na]
she	**նա** [na]
they (masc.)	**նրանք** [nrank]
they (fem.)	**նրանք** [nrank]
we	**մենք** [menq]
you (pl)	**դուք** [duq]
you (sg, form.)	**Դուք** [duq]

ENTRANCE	**ՄՈՒՏՔ** [mutq]
EXIT	**ԵԼՔ** [yelq]
OUT OF ORDER	**ՉԻ ԱՇԽԱՏՈՒՄ** [chi ashkhat'um]
CLOSED	**ՓԱԿ Է** [pak e]

OPEN	**ԲԱՑ Է** [bats e]
FOR WOMEN	**ԿԱՆԱՆՑ ՀԱՄԱՐ** [kan'ants ham'ar]
FOR MEN	**ՏՂԱՄԱՐԴԿԱՆՑ ՀԱՄԱՐ** [tghamardk'ants ham'ar]

TOPICAL VOCABULARY

This section contains more than 3,000 of the most important words.
The dictionary will provide invaluable assistance while traveling abroad, because frequently individual words are enough for you to be understood.
The dictionary includes a convenient transcription of each foreign word

T&P Books Publishing

VOCABULARY CONTENTS

T&P Books Publishing

BASIC CONCEPTS

T&P Books Publishing

1. Pronouns

I, me	ես	[es]
you	դու	[du]
he, she, it	նա	[na]
we	մենք	[meŋk]
you (to a group)	դուք	[duk]
they	նրանք	[nraŋk]

2. Greetings. Salutations

Hello! (fam.)	Բարև	[ba'rɛv]
Hello! (form.)	Բարև՛ ձեզ	[ba'rɛv 'dzɛz]
Good morning!	Բարի լո՛ւյս	[ba'ri 'lujs]
Good afternoon!	Բարի օ՛ր	[ba'ri 'or]
Good evening!	Բարի երեկո՛	[ba'ri jere'ko]
to say hello	բարևել	[bare'vel]
Hi! (hello)	Ողջո՛ւյն	[voh'ʤujn]
greeting (n)	ողջույն	[voh'ʤujn]
to greet (vt)	ողջունել	[vohʤu'nel]
How are you?	Ո՞նց են գործերդ	['vonts ɛn gor'tserd]
What's new?	Ի՞նչ նորություն	['intʃ noru'tsyn]
Bye-Bye! Goodbye!	Ցտեսությո՛ւն	['tsyn]
See you soon!	Մինչ նոր հանդիպո՛ւմ	['mintʃ 'nor andi'pum]
Farewell! (to a friend)	Մնաս բարո՛վ	[m'nas ba'rov]
Farewell! (form.)	Մնաք բարո՛վ	[m'nak ba'rov]
to say goodbye	հրաժեշտ տալ	[ɛra'ʒeʃt 'tal]
So long!	Առա՛յժմ	[a'rajʒm]
Thank you!	Շնորհակալությո՛ւն	[ʃnorakalu'tsyn]
Thank you very much!	Շատ շնորհակա՛լ եմ	['ʃʌt ʃnora'kal em]
You're welcome	Խնդրեմ	[hndrem]
Don't mention it!	Հոգ չէ	[og 'tʃə]
It was nothing	չարժե	[tʃar'ʒɛ]
Excuse me! (fam.)	Ներողությո՛ւն	[nerohu'tsyn]
Excuse me! (form.)	Ներեցե՛ք	[nere'tsek]
to excuse (forgive)	ներել	[ne'rel]
to apologize (vi)	ներողություն խնդրել	[nerohu'tsyn hnd'rel]
My apologies	Ներեցեք	[nere'tsek]

I'm sorry!	Ներեցե՛ք	[nere'tsek]
to forgive (vt)	ներել	[ne'rel]
please (adv)	խնդրում եմ	[hnd'rum em]
Don't forget!	Չմոռանա՛ք	[tʃmora'nak]
Certainly!	Իհա՛րկե	[i'arke]
Of course not!	Իհարկե ո՛չ	[i'arke 'votʃ]
Okay! (I agree)	Համաձա՛յն եմ	[ama'dzajn em]
That's enough!	Բավակա՛ն է	[bava'kan ɛ]

3. Questions

Who?	Ո՞վ	[ov]
What?	Ի՞նչ	[intʃ]
Where? (at, in)	Որտե՞ղ	[vor'teh]
Where (to)?	Ո՞ւր	[ur]
From where?	Որտեղի՞ց	[vorte'hits]
When?	Ե՞րբ	[erb]
Why? (What for?)	Ինչո՞ւ	[in'tʃu]
Why? (reason)	Ինչո՞ւ	[in'tʃu]
What for?	Ինչի՞ համար	[in'tʃi a'mar]
How? (in what way)	Ինչպե՞ս	[intʃ'pes]
What? (What kind of ...?)	Ինչպիսի՞	[intʃpi'si]
Which?	Ո՞րը	[vo'rɛ]
To whom?	Ո՞ւմ	[um]
About whom?	Ո՞ւմ մասին	['um ma'sin]
About what?	Ինչի՞ մասին	[in'tʃi ma'sin]
With whom?	Ո՞ւմ հետ	['um 'ɛt]
How many? How much?	քանի՞	[ka'ni]
Whose?	Ո՞ւմ	[um]

4. Prepositions

with (accompanied by)	... հետ	[ɛt]
without	առանց	[a'rants]
to (indicating direction)	մեջ	[medʒ]
about (talking ~ ...)	մասին	[ma'sin]
before (in time)	առաջ	[a'radʒ]
in front of ...	առաջ	[a'radʒ]
under (beneath, below)	տակ	[tak]
above (over)	վերևում	[vere'vum]
on (atop)	վրա	[vra]
from (off, out of)	... ից	[its]
of (made from)	... ից	[its]

in (e.g., ~ ten minutes)	... անց	[ants]
over (across the top of)	միջով	[mi'dʒov]

5. Function words. Adverbs. Part 1

Where? (at, in)	Որտե՞ղ	[vor'teh]
here (adv)	այստեղ	[ajs'teh]
there (adv)	այնտեղ	[ajn'teh]
somewhere (to be)	որևէ տեղ	[vore'vɛ 'teh]
nowhere (not anywhere)	ոչ մի տեղ	[votʃ mi 'teh]
by (near, beside)	... մոտ	[mot]
by the window	պատուհանի մոտ	[patua'ni 'mot]
Where (to)?	Ո՞ւր	[ur]
here (e.g., come ~!)	այստեղ	[ajs'teh]
there (e.g., to go ~)	այնտեղ	[ajn'teh]
from here (adv)	այստեղից	[ajste'hits]
from there (adv)	այնտեղից	[ajnte'hits]
close (adv)	մոտ	[mot]
far (adv)	հեռու	[ɛ'ru]
near (e.g., ~ Paris)	մոտ	[mot]
nearby (adv)	մոտակայքում	[motakaj'kum]
not far (adv)	մոտիկ	[mo'tik]
left (adj)	ձախ	[dzah]
on the left	ձախ կողմից	['dzah koh'mits]
to the left	դեպի ձախ	[de'pi 'dzah]
right (adj)	աջ	[adʒ]
on the right	աջ կողմից	['adʒ koh'mits]
to the right	դեպի աջ	[de'pi 'adʒ]
in front (adv)	առջևից	[ardʒe'vits]
front (as adj)	առջևի	[ardʒe'vi]
ahead (the kids ran ~)	առաջ	[a'radʒ]
behind (adv)	հետևում	[ɛte'vum]
from behind	հետևից	[ɛte'vits]
back (towards the rear)	հետ	[ɛt]
middle	մեջտեղ	[medʒ'teh]
in the middle	մեջտեղում	[medʒte'hum]
at the side	կողքից	[koh'kits]
everywhere (adv)	ամենուր	[ame'nur]
around (in all directions)	շուրջը	['ʃurdʒɛ]
from inside	միջից	[mi'dʒits]

somewhere (to go)	որևէ տեղ	[vore'vɛ 'teh]
straight (directly)	ուղիղ	[u'hih]
back (e.g., come ~)	ետ	[et]
from anywhere	որևէ տեղից	[vore'vɛ te'hiʦ]
from somewhere	ինչ-որ տեղից	['inʧ 'vor te'hiʦ]
firstly (adv)	առաջինը	[ara'ʤinɛ]
secondly (adv)	երկրորդը	[erk'rordɛ]
thirdly (adv)	երրորդը	[er'rordɛ]
suddenly (adv)	հանկարծակի	[aŋkar'ʦaki]
at first (at the beginning)	սկզբում	[skzbum]
for the first time	առաջին անգամ	[ara'ʤin a'ŋam]
long before ...	... շատ առաջ	['ʃʌt a'raʤ]
anew (over again)	կրկին	[krkin]
for good (adv)	ընդմիշտ	[ɪnd'miʃt]
never (adv)	երբեք	[er'bek]
again (adv)	նորից	[no'riʦ]
now (adv)	այժմ	[ajʒm]
often (adv)	հաճախ	[a'ʧah]
then (adv)	այն ժամանակ	['ajn ʒama'nak]
urgently (quickly)	շտապ	[ʃtap]
usually (adv)	սովորաբար	[sovora'bar]
by the way, ...	ի դեպ, ...	[i 'dep]
possible (that is ~)	հնարավոր է	[ɛnara'vor ɛ]
probably (adv)	հավանաբար	[avana'bar]
maybe (adv)	միգուցե	[migu'ʦe]
besides ...	բացի այդ, ...	[ba'ʦi 'ajd]
that's why ...	այդ պատճառով	['ajd paʧa'rov]
in spite of ...	չնայած ...	[ʧna'jaʦ]
thanks to ...	շնորհիվ ...	[ʃno'riv]
what (pron.)	ինչ	[inʧ]
that (conj.)	որ	[vor]
something	ինչ-որ բան	[inʧ vor 'ban]
anything (something)	որևէ բան	['vorevɛ 'ban]
nothing	ոչ մի բան	[voʧ mi 'ban]
who (pron.)	ով	[ov]
someone	ինչ-որ մեկը	['inʧ 'vor 'mekɪ]
somebody	որևէ մեկը	['vorevɛ 'mekɪ]
nobody	ոչ մեկ	[voʧ 'mek]
nowhere (a voyage to ~)	ոչ մի տեղ	[voʧ mi 'teh]
nobody's	ոչ մեկինը	['voʧ me'kinɪ]
somebody's	որևէ մեկինը	['vorevɛ me'kinɪ]
so (I'm ~ glad)	այնպես	[ajn'pes]
also (as well)	նմանապես	[nmana'pes]
too (as well)	նույնպես	['nujnpes]

6. Function words. Adverbs. Part 2

Why?	Ինչո՞ւ	[in'ʧu]
for some reason	չգիտես ինչու	[ʧgi'tes in'ʧu]
because ...	որովհետև, ...	[vorovɛ'tev]
for some purpose	ինչ-որ նպատակով	['inʧ 'vor npata'kov]
and	և	[ev]
or	կամ	[kam]
but	բայց	[bajʦ]
for (e.g., ~ me)	համար	[a'mar]
too (~ many people)	չափազանց	[ʧapa'zanʦ]
only (exclusively)	միայն	[mi'ajn]
exactly (adv)	ճիշտ	[ʧiʃt]
about (more or less)	մոտ	[mot]
approximately (adv)	մոտավորապես	[motavora'pes]
approximate (adj)	մոտավոր	[mota'vor]
almost (adv)	գրեթե	[g'rete]
the rest	մնացածը	[mna'ʦaʦɪ]
each (adj)	յուրաքանչյուր	[jurakan'ʧur]
any (no matter which)	ցանկացած	[ʦaŋka'ʦaʦ]
many, much (a lot of)	շատ	[ʃʌt]
many people	շատերը	[ʃʌ'terɪ]
all (everyone)	բոլորը	[bo'lorɪ]
in return for ...	ի փոխարեն ...	[i poha'ren]
in exchange (adv)	փոխարեն	[poha'ren]
by hand (made)	ձեռքով	[ʣer'kov]
hardly (negative opinion)	հազիվ թե	[a'ziv te]
probably (adv)	երևի	[ere'vi]
on purpose (intentionally)	դիտմամբ	[dit'mamb]
by accident (adv)	պատահաբար	[pata:'bar]
very (adv)	շատ	[ʃʌt]
for example (adv)	օրինակ	[ori'nak]
between	միջև	[mi'ʤev]
among	միջավայրում	[miʤavaj'rum]
so much (such a lot)	այնքան	[aj'ŋkan]
especially (adv)	հատկապես	[atka'pes]

NUMBERS. MISCELLANEOUS

T&P Books Publishing

7. Cardinal numbers. Part 1

0 zero	զրո	[zro]
1 one	մեկ	[mek]
2 two	երկու	[er'ku]
3 three	երեք	[e'rek]
4 four	չորս	[ʧors]
5 five	հինգ	[hiŋ]
6 six	վեց	[veʦ]
7 seven	յոթ	[jot]
8 eight	ութ	[ut]
9 nine	ինը	['inɛ]
10 ten	տաս	[tas]
11 eleven	տասնմեկ	[tasn'mek]
12 twelve	տասներկու	[tasner'ku]
13 thirteen	տասներեք	[tasne'rek]
14 fourteen	տասնչորս	[tasn'ʧors]
15 fifteen	տասնհինգ	[tas'niŋ]
16 sixteen	տասնվեց	[tasn'veʦ]
17 seventeen	տասնյոթ	[tasn'jot]
18 eighteen	տասնութ	[tas'nut]
19 nineteen	տասնինը	[tas'ninɛ]
20 twenty	քսան	[ksan]
21 twenty-one	քսանմեկ	[ksan'mek]
22 twenty-two	քսաներկու	[ksaner'ku]
23 twenty-three	քսաներեք	[ksane'rek]
30 thirty	երեսուն	[ere'sun]
31 thirty-one	երեսունմեկ	[eresun'mek]
32 thirty-two	երեսուներկու	[eresuner'ku]
33 thirty-three	երեսուներեք	[eresune'rek]
40 forty	քառասուն	[kara'sun]
41 forty-one	քառասունմեկ	[karasun'mek]
42 forty-two	քառասուներկու	[karasuner'ku]
43 forty-three	քառասուներեք	[karasune'rek]
50 fifty	հիսուն	[i'sun]
51 fifty-one	հիսունմեկ	[isun'mek]
52 fifty-two	հիսուներկու	[isuner'ku]
53 fifty-three	հիսուներեք	[isune'rek]
60 sixty	վաթսուն	[va'ʦun]

61 sixty-one	վաթսունմեկ	[vaʦun'mek]
62 sixty-two	վաթսուներկու	[vaʦuner'ku]
63 sixty-three	վաթսուներեք	[vaʦune'rek]
70 seventy	յոթանասուն	[jotana'sun]
71 seventy-one	յոթանասունմեկ	[jotanasun'mek]
72 seventy-two	յոթանասուներկու	[jotanasuner'ku]
73 seventy-three	յոթանասուներեք	[jotanasune'rek]
80 eighty	ութսուն	[u'ʦun]
81 eighty-one	ութսունմեկ	[uʦun'mek]
82 eighty-two	ութսուներկու	[uʦuner'ku]
83 eighty-three	ութսուներեք	[uʦune'rek]
90 ninety	իննսուն	[iŋ'sun]
91 ninety-one	իննսունմեկ	[iŋsun'mek]
92 ninety-two	իննսուներկու	[iŋsuner'ku]
93 ninety-three	իննսուներեք	[iŋsune'rek]

8. Cardinal numbers. Part 2

100 one hundred	հարյուր	[ar'jur]
200 two hundred	երկու հարյուր	[er'ku ar'jur]
300 three hundred	երեք հարյուր	[e'rek ar'jur]
400 four hundred	չորս հարյուր	['ʧors ar'jur]
500 five hundred	հինգ հարյուր	['hiŋ ar'jur]
600 six hundred	վեց հարյուր	['veʦ ar'jur]
700 seven hundred	յոթ հարյուր	['jot ar'jur]
800 eight hundred	ութ հարյուր	['ut ar'jur]
900 nine hundred	ինը հարյուր	['inɛ ar'jur]
1000 one thousand	հազար	[a'zar]
2000 two thousand	երկու հազար	[er'ku a'zar]
3000 three thousand	երեք հազար	[e'rek a'zar]
10000 ten thousand	տաս հազար	['tas a'zar]
one hundred thousand	հարյուր հազար	[ar'jur a'zar]
million	միլիոն	[mili'on]
billion	միլիարդ	[mili'ard]

9. Ordinal numbers

first (adj)	առաջին	[ara'ʤin]
second (adj)	երկրորդ	[erk'rord]
third (adj)	երրորդ	[er'rord]
fourth (adj)	չորրորդ	[ʧor'rord]
fifth (adj)	հինգերորդ	['hiŋerord]
sixth (adj)	վեցերորդ	['veʦerord]

seventh (adj)	**յոթերորդ**	['joterord]
eighth (adj)	**ութերորդ**	['uterord]
ninth (adj)	**իններորդ**	['iŋerord]
tenth (adj)	**տասներորդ**	['tɑsnerord]

COLOURS. UNITS OF MEASUREMENT

T&P Books Publishing

10. Colors

color	գույն	[gujn]
shade (tint)	երանգ	[e'raŋ]
hue	գուներանգ	[gunɛ'raŋ]
rainbow	ծիածան	[ʦia'ʦan]
white (adj)	սպիտակ	[spi'tak]
black (adj)	սև	[sev]
gray (adj)	մոխրագույն	[mohra'gujn]
green (adj)	կանաչ	[ka'naʧ]
yellow (adj)	դեղին	[de'hin]
red (adj)	կարմիր	[kar'mir]
blue (adj)	կապույտ	[ka'pujt]
light blue (adj)	երկնագույն	[erkna'gujn]
pink (adj)	վարդագույն	[varda'gujn]
orange (adj)	նարնջագույն	[narnʤa'gujn]
violet (adj)	մանուշակագույն	[manuʃʌka'gujn]
brown (adj)	շագանակագույն	[ʃʌganaka'gujn]
golden (adj)	ոսկե	[vos'ke]
silvery (adj)	արծաթագույն	[arʦata'gujn]
beige (adj)	բեժ	[beʒ]
cream (adj)	կրեմագույն	[krema'gujn]
turquoise (adj)	փիրուզագույն	[piruza'gujn]
cherry red (adj)	բալագույն	[bala'gujn]
lilac (adj)	բաց մանուշակագույն	['baʦ manuʃʌka'gujn]
crimson (adj)	մորեգույն	[more'gujn]
light (adj)	բաց	[baʦ]
dark (adj)	մուգ	[mug]
bright, vivid (adj)	վառ	[var]
colored (pencils)	գունավոր	[guna'vor]
color (e.g., ~ film)	գունավոր	[guna'vor]
black-and-white (adj)	սև ու սպիտակ	['sev u spi'tak]
plain (one-colored)	միագույն	[mia'gujn]
multicolored (adj)	գույնզգույն	[gujnz'gujn]

11. Units of measurement

weight	քաշ	[kaʃ]
length	երկարություն	[erkaru'ʦyn]

width	լայնություն	[lajnu'tsyn]
height	բարձրություն	[bardzru'tsyn]
depth	խորություն	[horu'tsyn]
volume	ծավալ	[tsa'val]
area	մակերես	[make'res]
gram	գրամ	[gram]
milligram	միլիգրամ	[milig'ram]
kilogram	կիլոգրամ	[kilog'ram]
ton	տոննա	['toŋa]
pound	ֆունտ	[funt]
ounce	ունցիա	['untsija]
meter	մետր	[metr]
millimeter	միլիմետր	[mili'metr]
centimeter	սանտիմետր	[santi'metr]
kilometer	կիլոմետր	[kilo'metr]
mile	մղոն	[mhon]
inch	դյույմ	[dyjm]
foot	ֆութ	[fut]
yard	յարդ	[jard]
square meter	քառակուսի մետր	[karaku'si 'metr]
hectare	հեկտար	[ɛk'tar]
liter	լիտր	[litr]
degree	աստիճան	[asti'tʃan]
volt	վոլտ	[voʎt]
ampere	ամպեր	[am'per]
horsepower	ձիաուժ	[dzia'uʒ]
quantity	քանակ	[ka'nak]
a little bit of ...	մի փոքր ...	['mi pokr]
half	կես	[kes]
dozen	դյուժին	[dy'ʒin]
piece (item)	հատ	[at]
size	չափս	[tʃaps]
scale (map ~)	մասշտաբ	[masʃ'tab]
minimal (adj)	նվազագույն	[nvaza'gujn]
the smallest (adj)	փոքրագույն	[pokra'gujn]
medium (adj)	միջին	[mi'dʒin]
maximal (adj)	առավելագույն	[aravela'gujn]
the largest (adj)	մեծագույն	[metsa'gujn]

12. Containers

canning jar (glass ~)	բանկա	[ba'ŋka]
can	տարա	[ta'ra]

bucket	դույլ	[dujl]
barrel	տակառ	[ta'kar]
wash basin (e.g., plastic ~)	թաս	[tas]
tank (100 - 200L water ~)	բաք	[bak]
hip flask	տափակաշիշ	[tapaka'ʃiʃ]
jerrycan	թիթեղ	[ti'teh]
tank (e.g., tank car)	ցիստեռն	[ʦis'tern]
mug	գավաթ	[ga'vat]
cup (of coffee, etc.)	բաժակ	[ba'ʒak]
saucer	պնակ	[pnak]
glass (tumbler)	բաժակ	[ba'ʒak]
wine glass	գավաթ	[ga'vat]
stock pot (soup pot)	կաթսա	[ka'ʦa]
bottle (~ of wine)	շիշ	[ʃiʃ]
neck (of the bottle, etc.)	բերան	[be'ran]
carafe	գրաֆին	[gra'fin]
pitcher	սափոր	[sa'por]
vessel (container)	անոթ	[a'not]
pot (crock, stoneware ~)	կճուճ	[kʧuʧ]
vase	վազա	['vaza]
bottle (perfume ~)	սրվակ	[srvak]
vial, small bottle	սրվակիկ	[srva'kik]
tube (of toothpaste)	պարկուճ	[par'kuʧ]
sack (bag)	պարկ	[park]
bag (paper ~, plastic ~)	տոպրակ	[top'rak]
pack (of cigarettes, etc.)	տուփ	[tup]
box (e.g., shoebox)	տուփ	[tup]
crate	դարակ	[da'rak]
basket	զամբյուղ	[zam'byh]

MAIN VERBS

T&P Books Publishing

13. The most important verbs. Part 1

to advise (vt)	խորհուրդ տալ	[ho'rurd 'tal]
to agree (say yes)	համաձայնվել	[amadzajn'vel]
to answer (vi, vt)	պատասխանել	[patasha'nel]
to apologize (vi)	ներողություն խնդրել	[nerohu'tsyn hnd'rel]
to arrive (vi)	ժամանել	[ʒama'nel]
to ask (~ oneself)	հարցնել	[arts'nel]
to ask (~ sb to do sth)	խնդրել	[hndrel]
to be (vi)	լինել	[li'nel]
to be afraid	վախենալ	[vahe'nal]
to be hungry	ուզենալ ուտել	[uze'nal u'tel]
to be interested in ...	հետաքրքրվել	[ɛtakrkr'vel]
to be needed	պետք լինել	['petk li'nel]
to be surprised	զարմանալ	[zarma'nal]
to be thirsty	ուզենալ խմել	[uze'nal h'mel]
to begin (vt)	սկսել	[sksel]
to belong to ...	պատկանել	[patka'nel]
to boast (vi)	պարծենալ	[partse'nal]
to break (split into pieces)	կոտրել	[kot'rel]
to call (~ for help)	կանչել	[kan'tʃel]
can (v aux)	կարողանալ	[karoha'nal]
to catch (vt)	բռնել	[brnel]
to change (vt)	փոխել	[po'hel]
to choose (select)	ընտրել	[ɪnt'rel]
to come down (the stairs)	իջնել	[idʒ'nel]
to compare (vt)	համեմատել	[amema'tel]
to complain (vi, vt)	գանգատվել	[gaŋat'vel]
to confuse (mix up)	շփոթել	[ʃpo'tel]
to continue (vt)	շարունակել	[ʃʌruna'kel]
to control (vt)	վերահսկել	[veraɛs'kel]
to cook (dinner)	պատրաստել	[patras'tel]
to cost (vt)	արժենալ	[arʒe'nal]
to count (add up)	հաշվել	[aʃ'vel]
to count on ...	հույս դնել ... վրա	[ujs dnel v'ra]
to create (vt)	ստեղծել	[steh'tsel]
to cry (weep)	լացել	[la'tsel]

14. The most important verbs. Part 2

to deceive (vi, vt)	խաբել	[ha'bel]
to decorate (tree, street)	զարդարել	[zarda'rel]
to defend (a country, etc.)	պաշտպանել	[paʃtpa'nel]
to demand (request firmly)	պահանջել	[pa:n'ʤel]
to dig (vt)	փորել	[po'rel]
to discuss (vt)	քննարկել	[kŋar'kel]
to do (vt)	անել	[a'nel]
to doubt (have doubts)	կասկածել	[kaska'ʦel]
to drop (let fall)	վայր գցել	['vajr gʦel]
to enter (room, house, etc.)	մտնել	[mtnel]
to exist (vi)	գոյություն ունենալ	[goju'ʦyn une'nal]
to expect (foresee)	կանխատեսել	[kanhate'sel]
to explain (vt)	բացատրել	[baʦat'rel]
to fall (vi)	ընկնել	[ɛŋk'nel]
to find (vt)	գտնել	[gtnel]
to finish (vt)	ավարտել	[avar'tel]
to fly (vi)	թռչել	[trʧel]
to follow ... (come after)	գնալ ... հետևից	[gnal ɛte'viʦ]
to forget (vi, vt)	մոռանալ	[mora'nal]
to forgive (vt)	ներել	[ne'rel]
to give (vt)	տալ	[tal]
to give a hint	ակնարկել	[aknar'kel]
to go (on foot)	գնալ	[gnal]
to go for a swim	լողալ	[lo'hal]
to go out (for dinner, etc.)	դուրս գալ	['durs gal]
to guess (the answer)	գուշակել	[guʃʌ'kel]
to have (vt)	ունենալ	[une'nal]
to have breakfast	նախաճաշել	[nahaʧa'ʃəl]
to have dinner	ընթրել	[ɪnt'rel]
to have lunch	ճաշել	[ʧa'ʃəl]
to hear (vt)	լսել	[lsel]
to help (vt)	օգնել	[og'nel]
to hide (vt)	թաքցնել	[takʦ'nel]
to hope (vi, vt)	հուսալ	[u'sal]
to hunt (vi, vt)	որս անել	['vors a'nel]
to hurry (vi)	շտապել	[ʃta'pel]

15. The most important verbs. Part 3

to inform (vt)	տեղեկացնել	[tehekaʦ'nel]
to insist (vi, vt)	պնդել	[pndel]

to insult (vt)	վիրավորել	[viravo'rel]
to invite (vt)	հրավիրել	[ɛravi'rel]
to joke (vi)	կատակել	[kata'kel]
to keep (vt)	պահպանել	[pahpa'nel]
to keep silent	լռել	[lrel]
to kill (vt)	սպանել	[spa'nel]
to know (sb)	ճանաչել	[ʧana'ʧel]
to know (sth)	իմանալ	[ima'nal]
to laugh (vi)	ծիծաղել	[ʦiʦa'hel]
to liberate (city, etc.)	ազատագրել	[azatag'rel]
to like (I like ...)	դուր գալ	['dur gal]
to look for ... (search)	փնտրել	[pntrel]
to love (sb)	սիրել	[si'rel]
to make a mistake	սխալվել	[shal'vel]
to manage, to run	ղեկավարել	[hekava'rel]
to mean (signify)	նշանակել	[nʃʌna'kel]
to mention (talk about)	հիշատակել	[iʃʌta'kel]
to miss (school, etc.)	բաց թողնել	['baʦ toh'nel]
to notice (see)	նկատել	[ŋka'tel]
to object (vi, vt)	հակաճառել	[akaʧa'rel]
to observe (see)	հետևել	[ɛte'vel]
to open (vt)	բացել	[ba'ʦel]
to order (meal, etc.)	պատվիրել	[patvi'rel]
to order (mil.)	հրամայել	[ɛrama'jel]
to own (possess)	ունենալ	[une'nal]
to participate (vi)	մասնակցել	[masnak'ʦel]
to pay (vi, vt)	վճարել	[vʧa'rel]
to permit (vt)	թույլատրել	[tujlat'rel]
to plan (vt)	պլանավորել	[planavo'rel]
to play (children)	խաղալ	[ha'hal]
to pray (vi, vt)	աղոթել	[aho'tel]
to prefer (vt)	նախընտրել	[nahɛnt'rel]
to promise (vt)	խոստանալ	[hosta'nal]
to pronounce (vt)	արտասանել	[artasa'nel]
to propose (vt)	առաջարկել	[araʤar'kel]
to punish (vt)	պատժել	[pat'ʒel]

16. The most important verbs. Part 4

to read (vi, vt)	կարդալ	[kar'dal]
to recommend (vt)	երաշխավորել	[eraʃhavo'rel]
to refuse (vi, vt)	հրաժարվել	[ɛraʒar'vel]
to regret (be sorry)	ափսոսալ	[apso'sal]
to rent (sth from sb)	վարձել	[var'ʣel]

to repeat (say again)	կրկնել	[krknel]
to reserve, to book	ամրագրել	[amrag'rel]
to run (vi)	վազել	[va'zel]
to save (rescue)	փրկել	[prkel]
to say (~ thank you)	ասել	[a'sel]
to scold (vt)	կշտամբել	[kʃtam'bel]
to see (vt)	տեսնել	[tes'nel]
to sell (vt)	վաճառել	[vatʃa'rel]
to send (vt)	ուղարկել	[uhar'kel]
to shoot (vi)	կրակել	[kra'kel]
to shout (vi)	բղավել	[bha'vel]
to show (vt)	ցույց տալ	['tsujts tal]
to sign (document)	ստորագրել	[storag'rel]
to sit down (vi)	նստել	[nstel]
to smile (vi)	ժպտալ	[ʒptal]
to speak (vi, vt)	խոսել	[ho'sel]
to steal (money, etc.)	գողանալ	[goha'nal]
to stop (for pause, etc.)	կանգ առնել	['kaŋ ar'nel]
to stop (please ~ calling me)	դադարեցնել	[dadarets'nel]
to study (vt)	ուսումնասիրել	[usumnasi'rel]
to swim (vi)	լողալ	[lo'hal]
to take (vt)	վերցնել	[verts'nel]
to think (vi, vt)	մտածել	[mta'tsel]
to threaten (vt)	սպառնալ	[spar'nal]
to touch (with hands)	ձեռք տալ	['dzerk tal]
to translate (vt)	թարգմանել	[targma'nel]
to trust (vt)	վստահել	[vsta'ɛl]
to try (attempt)	փորձել	[por'dzel]
to turn (e.g., ~ left)	թեքվել	[tɛk'vel]
to underestimate (vt)	թերագնահատել	[teragna:'tel]
to understand (vt)	հասկանալ	[aska'nal]
to unite (vt)	միավորել	[miavo'rel]
to wait (vt)	սպասել	[spa'sel]
to want (wish, desire)	ուզենալ	[uze'nal]
to warn (vt)	զգուշացնել	[zguʃʌts'nel]
to work (vi)	աշխատել	[aʃha'tel]
to write (vt)	գրել	[grel]
to write down	գրառել	[gra'rel]

TIME. CALENDAR

T&P Books Publishing

17. Weekdays

Monday	երկուշաբթի	[erkuʃʌb'ti]
Tuesday	երեքշաբթի	[erekʃʌb'ti]
Wednesday	չորեքշաբթի	[ʧorekʃʌb'ti]
Thursday	հինգշաբթի	[iŋʃʌb'ti]
Friday	ուրբաթ	[ur'bat]
Saturday	շաբաթ	[ʃʌ'bat]
Sunday	կիրակի	[kira'ki]
today (adv)	այսօր	[aj'sor]
tomorrow (adv)	վաղը	['vahɪ]
the day after tomorrow	վաղը չէ մյուս օրը	['vahɪ 'ʧe 'mys 'orɪ]
yesterday (adv)	երեկ	[e'rek]
the day before yesterday	նախանցյալ օրը	[nahan'ʦʲal 'orɪ]
day	օր	[or]
working day	աշխատանքային օր	[aʃhataŋka'jɪn 'or]
public holiday	տոնական օր	[tona'kan 'or]
day off	հանգստյան օր	[aŋs'tʲan 'or]
weekend	շաբաթ, կիրակի	[ʃʌ'bat], [kira'ki]
all day long	ամբողջ օր	[am'bohʤ 'or]
the next day (adv)	մյուս օրը	['mys 'orɪ]
two days ago	երկու օր առաջ	[er'ku 'or a'raʤ]
the day before	նախորդ օրը	[na'hord 'orɪ]
daily (adj)	ամենօրյա	[ameno'rʲa]
every day (adv)	ամեն օր	[a'men 'or]
week	շաբաթ	[ʃʌ'bat]
last week (adv)	անցյալ շաբաթ	[an'ʦʲal ʃʌ'bat]
next week (adv)	հաջորդ շաբաթ	[a'ʤort 'orɪ]
weekly (adj)	շաբաթական	[ʃʌbata'kan]
every week (adv)	շաբաթական	[ʃʌbata'kan]
twice a week	շաբաթը երկու անգամ	[ʃʌ'batɪ er'ku a'ŋam]
every Tuesday	ամեն երեքշաբթի	[a'men erekʃʌb'ti]

18. Hours. Day and night

morning	առավոտ	[ara'vot]
in the morning	առավոտյան	[aravo'tʲan]
noon, midday	կեսօր	[ke'sor]
in the afternoon	ճաշից հետո	[ʧa'ʃiʦ ɛ'to]
evening	երեկո	[ere'ko]

in the evening	երեկոյան	[ereko'jan]
night	գիշեր	[gi'ʃər]
at night	գիշերը	[gi'ʃərı]
midnight	կեսգիշեր	[kesgi'ʃər]
second	վայրկյան	[vajr'kʲan]
minute	րոպե	[ro'pɛ]
hour	ժամ	[ʒam]
half an hour	կես ժամ	[kes 'ʒam]
a quarter-hour	քառորդ ժամ	[ka'rord 'ʒam]
fifteen minutes	տասնհինգ րոպե	[tas'niŋ ro'pɛ]
24 hours	օր	[or]
sunrise	արևածագ	[areva'ʦag]
dawn	արևածագ	[areva'ʦag]
early morning	վաղ առավոտ	['vah ara'vot]
sunset	մայրամուտ	[majra'mut]
early in the morning	վաղ առավոտյան	['vah aravo'tʲan]
this morning	այսօր առավոտյան	[aj'sor aravo'tʲan]
tomorrow morning	վաղը առավոտյան	['vahı aravo'tʲan]
this afternoon	այսօր ցերեկը	[aj'sor ʦe'rekı]
in the afternoon	ճաշից հետո	[ʧa'ʃiʦ ɛ'to]
tomorrow afternoon	վաղը ճաշից հետո	['vahı ʧa'ʃiʦ ɛ'to]
tonight (this evening)	այսօր երեկոյան	[aj'sor ereko'jan]
tomorrow night	վաղը երեկոյան	['vahı ereko'jan]
at 3 o'clock sharp	ուղիղ ժամը երեքին	[u'hih 'ʒamı ere'kin]
about 4 o'clock	մոտ ժամը չորսին	['mot 'ʒamı ʧor'sin]
by 12 o'clock	մոտ ժամը տասներկուսին	['mot 'ʒamı tasnerku'sin]
in 20 minutes	քսան րոպեից	[k'san ropɛ'iʦ]
in an hour	մեկ ժամից	['mek ʒa'miʦ]
on time (adv)	ժամանակին	[ʒamana'kin]
a quarter of ...	տասնհինգ պակաս	[tas'niŋ pa'kas]
within an hour	մեկ ժամվա ընթացքում	['mek ʒam'va ıntaʦ'kum]
every 15 minutes	տասնհինգ րոպեն մեկ	[tas'niŋ ro'pen 'mek]
round the clock	ողջ օրը	['vohʤ 'orı]

19. Months. Seasons

January	հունվար	[un'var]
February	փետրվար	[petr'var]
March	մարտ	[mart]
April	ապրիլ	[ap'ril]
May	մայիս	[ma'jıs]

June	**հունիս**	[u'nis]
July	**հուլիս**	[u'lis]
August	**օգոստոս**	[ogos'tos]
September	**սեպտեմբեր**	[septem'ber]
October	**հոկտեմբեր**	[oktem'ber]
November	**նոյեմբեր**	[noem'ber]
December	**դեկտեմբեր**	[dektem'ber]
spring	**գարուն**	[ga'run]
in spring	**գարնանը**	[gar'nanı]
spring (as adj)	**գարնանային**	[garnana'jın]
summer	**ամառ**	[a'mar]
in summer	**ամռանը**	[am'ranı]
summer (as adj)	**ամառային**	[amara'jın]
fall	**աշուն**	[a'ʃun]
in fall	**աշնանը**	[aʃ'nanı]
fall (as adj)	**աշնանային**	[aʃnana'jın]
winter	**ձմեռ**	[ʣmer]
in winter	**ձմռանը**	[ʣm'ranı]
winter (as adj)	**ձմեռային**	[ʣmera'jın]
month	**ամիս**	[a'mis]
this month	**այս ամիս**	['ajs a'mis]
next month	**մյուս ամիս**	['mys a'mis]
last month	**անցյալ ամիս**	[an'ʦʲal a'mis]
a month ago	**մեկ ամիս առաջ**	['mek a'mis a'raʤ]
in a month (a month later)	**մեկ ամիս հետո**	['mek a'mis ɛ'to]
in 2 months (2 months later)	**երկու ամիս հետո**	[er'ku a'mis ɛ'to]
the whole month	**ամբողջ ամիս**	[am'bohʤ a'mis]
all month long	**ողջ ամիս**	['vohʤ a'mis]
monthly (~ magazine)	**ամսական**	[amsa'kan]
monthly (adv)	**ամեն ամիս**	[a'men a'mis]
every month	**ամեն ամիս**	[a'men a'mis]
twice a month	**ամսական երկու անգամ**	[amsa'kan er'ku a'ŋam]
year	**տարի**	[ta'ri]
this year	**այս տարի**	['ajs ta'ri]
next year	**մյուս տարի**	['mys ta'ri]
last year	**անցյալ տարի**	[an'ʦʲal ta'ri]
a year ago	**մեկ տարի առաջ**	['mek ta'ri a'raʤ]
in a year	**մեկ տարի անց**	['mek ta'ri 'anʦ]
in two years	**երկու տարի անց**	[er'ku ta'ri 'anʦ]
the whole year	**ամբողջ տարի**	[am'bohʤ ta'ri]
all year long	**ողջ տարի**	['vohʤ ta'ri]
every year	**ամեն տարի**	[a'men ta'ri]

annual (adj)	**տարեկան**	[tare'kan]
annually (adv)	**ամեն տարի**	[a'men ta'ri]
4 times a year	**տարեկան չորս անգամ**	[tare'kan 'ʧors a'ŋam]
date (e.g., today's ~)	**ամսաթիվ**	[amsa'tiv]
date (e.g., ~ of birth)	**ամսաթիվ**	[amsa'tiv]
calendar	**օրացույց**	[ora'ʦujʦ]
half a year	**կես տարի**	['kes ta'ri]
six months	**կիսամյակ**	[kisa'mʲak]
season (summer, etc.)	**սեզոն**	[se'zon]
century	**դար**	[dar]

TRAVEL. HOTEL

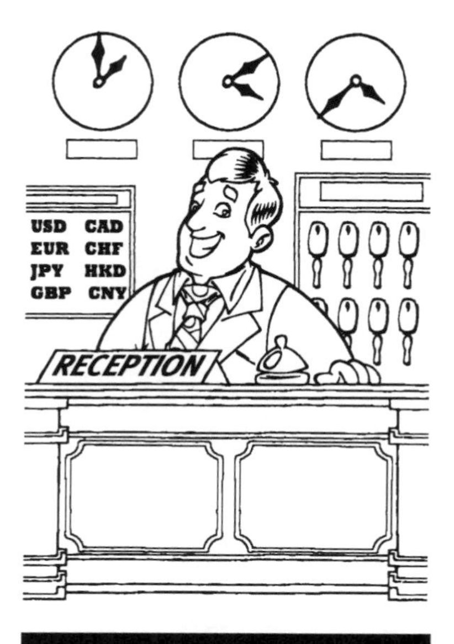

T&P Books Publishing

20. Trip. Travel

tourism, travel	զբոսաշրջություն	[zbosaʃrʤu'ʦyn]
tourist	զբոսաշրջիկ	[zbosaʃr'ʤik]
trip, voyage	ճանապարհորդություն	[ʧanaparordu'ʦyn]
adventure	արկած	[ar'kaʦ]
trip, journey	ուղևորություն	[uhevoru'ʦyn]
vacation	արձակուրդ	[arʣa'kurd]
to be on vacation	արձակուրդի մեջ լինել	[arʣakur'di 'meʤ li'nel]
rest	հանգիստ	[a'ŋist]
train	գնացք	[gnaʦk]
by train	գնացքով	[gnaʦ'kov]
airplane	ինքնաթիռ	[iŋkna'tir]
by airplane	ինքնաթիռով	[iŋknati'rov]
by car	ավտոմեքենայով	[avtomekena'jov]
by ship	նավով	[na'vov]
luggage	ուղեբեռ	[uhe'ber]
suitcase	ճամպրուկ	[ʧamp'ruk]
luggage cart	սայլակ	[saj'lak]
passport	անձնագիր	[anʣna'gir]
visa	վիզա	['viza]
ticket	տոմս	[toms]
air ticket	ավիատոմս	[avia'toms]
guidebook	ուղեցույց	[uhe'ʦujʦ]
map (tourist ~)	քարտեզ	[kar'tez]
area (rural ~)	տեղանք	[te'haŋk]
place, site	տեղ	[teh]
exotica (n)	էկզոտիկա	[ɛk'zotika]
exotic (adj)	էկզոտիկ	[ɛkzo'tik]
amazing (adj)	զարմանահրաշ	[zarmanaɛ'raʃ]
group	խումբ	[humb]
excursion, sightseeing tour	էքսկուրսիա	[ɛks'kursia]
guide (person)	էքսկուրսավար	[ɛkskursa'var]

21. Hotel

hotel	հյուրանոց	[ʒura'noʦ]
motel	մոթել	[mo'tel]

three-star	երեք աստղանի	[e'rek astha'ni]
five-star	հինգ աստղանի	['iŋ astha'ni]
to stay (in hotel, etc.)	կանգ առնել	['kaŋ ar'nel]
room	համար	[a'mar]
single room	մեկտեղանի համար	[mekteha'ni a'mar]
double room	երկտեղանի համար	[erkteha'ni a'mar]
to book a room	համար ամրագրել	[a'mar amrag'rel]
half board	կիսագիշերօթիկ	[kisagiʃəro'tik]
full board	լրիվ գիշերօթիկ	[l'riv giʃəro'tik]
with bath	լոգարանով	[logara'nov]
with shower	դուշով	[du'ʃov]
satellite television	արբանյակային հեռուստատեսություն	[arbaɲaka'jɪn ɛrustatesu'ʦyn]
air-conditioner	օդորակիչ	[odora'kiʧ]
towel	սրբիչ	[srbiʧ]
key	բանալի	[bana'li]
administrator	ադմինիստրատոր	[administ'rator]
chambermaid	սպասավորուհի	[spasavoru'i]
porter, bellboy	բեռնակիր	[berna'kir]
doorman	դռնապահ	[drna'pa]
restaurant	ռեստորան	[resto'ran]
pub, bar	բար	[bar]
breakfast	նախաճաշ	[naha'ʧaʃ]
dinner	ընթրիք	[ɪnt'rik]
buffet	շվեդական սեղան	[ʃveda'kan se'han]
elevator	վերելակ	[vere'lak]
DO NOT DISTURB	ՉԱՆՀԱՆԳՍՏԱՑՆԵԼ	[ʧanaŋstaʦ'nel]
NO SMOKING	Չ՛ԾԽԵԼ	[ʧʦ'hel]

22. Sightseeing

monument	արձան	[ar'ʣan]
fortress	ամրոց	[am'roʦ]
palace	պալատ	[pa'lat]
castle	դղյակ	[dɦak]
tower	աշտարակ	[aʃta'rak]
mausoleum	դամբարան	[damba'ran]
architecture	ճարտարապետություն	[ʧartarapetu'ʦyn]
medieval (adj)	միջնադարյան	[miʤnada'rʲan]
ancient (adj)	հինավուրց	[ina'vurʦ]
national (adj)	ազգային	[azga'jɪn]
well-known (adj)	հայտնի	[ajt'ni]
tourist	զբոսաշրջիկ	[zbosaʃr'ʤik]

guide (person)	գիդ	[gid]
excursion, sightseeing tour	էքսկուրսիա	[ɛks'kursia]
to show (vt)	ցույց տալ	['tsujts tal]
to tell (vt)	պատմել	[pat'mel]
to find (vt)	գտնել	[gtnel]
to get lost (lose one's way)	կորել	[ko'rel]
map (e.g., subway ~)	սխեմա	[s'hema]
map (e.g., city ~)	քարտեզ	[kar'tez]
souvenir, gift	հուշանվեր	[uʃʌn'ver]
gift shop	հուշանվերների խանութ	[uʃʌnverne'ri ha'nut]
to take pictures	լուսանկարել	[lusaŋka'rel]
to have one's picture taken	լուսանկարվել	[lusaŋkar'vel]

TRANSPORTATION

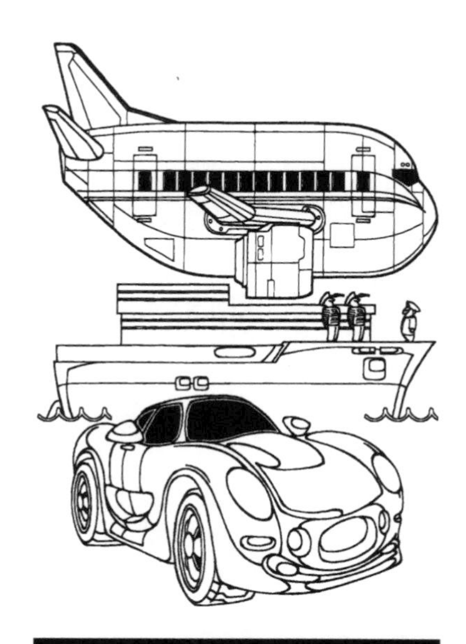

T&P Books Publishing

23. Airport

airport	օդանավակայան	[odanavaka'jan]
airplane	ինքնաթիռ	[iŋkna'tir]
airline	ավիաընկերություն	[aviaıŋkeru'tsyn]
air traffic controller	դիսպետչեր	[dispe'tʃer]
departure	թռիչք	[tritʃk]
arrival	ժամանում	[ʒama'num]
to arrive (by plane)	ժամանել	[ʒama'nel]
departure time	թռիչքի ժամանակը	[tritʃ'ki ʒama'nakı]
arrival time	ժամանման ժամանակը	[ʒaman'man ʒama'nakı]
to be delayed	ուշանալ	[uʃʌ'nal]
flight delay	թռիչքի ուշացում	[tritʃ'ki uʃʌ'tsum]
information board	տեղեկատվական վահանակ	[tehekatva'kan va:'nak]
information	տեղեկատվություն	[tehekatvu'tsyn]
to announce (vt)	հայտարարել	[ajtara'rel]
flight (e.g., next ~)	ռեյս	[rejs]
customs	մաքսատուն	[maksa'tun]
customs officer	մաքսավոր	[maksa'vor]
customs declaration	հայտարարագիր	[ajtarara'gir]
to fill out the declaration	հայտարարագիր լրացնել	[ajtarara'gir Irats'nel]
passport control	անձնագրային ստուգում	[andznagra'jın stu'gum]
luggage	ուղեբեռ	[uhe'ber]
hand luggage	ձեռքի ուղեբեռ	[dzer'ki uhe'ber]
Lost Luggage Desk	ուղեբեռի որոնում	[uhebe'ri voro'num]
luggage cart	սայլակ	[saj'lak]
landing	վայրէջք	[vaj'redʒk]
landing strip	վայրէջքի ուղի	[vajredʒ'ki u'hi]
to land (vi)	վայրէջք կատարել	[vaj'redʒk kata'rel]
airstairs	օդանավասանդուղք	[odanavasan'duhk]
check-in	գրանցում	[gran'tsum]
check-in desk	գրանցասեղան	[grantsase'han]
to check-in (vi)	գրանցվել	[grants'vel]
boarding pass	տեղակտրոն	[tehakt'ron]
departure gate	ելք	[elk]
transit	տարանցիկ չվերթ	[taran'tsik tʃ'vert]

to wait (vt)	սպասել	[spa'sel]
departure lounge	սպասասրահ	[spasas'ra]
to see off	ճանապարհել	[ʧanapa'rel]
to say goodbye	հրաժեշտ տալ	[ɛra'ʒeʃt 'tal]

24. Airplane

airplane	ինքնաթիռ	[iŋkna'tir]
air ticket	ավիատոմս	[avia'toms]
airline	ավիաընկերություն	[aviaɪŋkeru'ʦyn]
airport	օդանավակայան	[odanavaka'jan]
supersonic (adj)	գերձայնային	[gerʣajna'jɪn]
captain	օդանավի հրամանատար	[odana'vi ɛramana'tar]
crew	անձնակազմ	[anʣna'kazm]
pilot	օդաչու	[oda'ʧu]
flight attendant	ուղեկցորդուհի	[uhekʦordu'i]
navigator	ղեկապետ	[heka'pet]
wings	թևեր	[te'ver]
tail	պոչ	[poʧ]
cockpit	խցիկ	[hʦik]
engine	շարժիչ	[ʃʌr'ʒiʧ]
undercarriage (landing gear)	շասսի	[ʃʌs'si]
turbine	տուրբին	[tur'bin]
propeller	պրոպելլեր	[propel'ler]
black box	սև արկղ	[sev 'arkh]
yoke (control column)	ղեկանիվ	[heka'niv]
fuel	վառելիք	[vare'lik]
safety card	ձեռնարկ	[ʣer'nark]
oxygen mask	թթվածնային դիմակ	[ttvaʦna'jɪn di'mak]
uniform	համազգեստ	[amaz'gest]
life vest	փրկագոտի	[prkago'ti]
parachute	պարաշյուտ	[para'ʃyt]
takeoff	թռիչք	[triʧk]
to take off (vi)	թռնել	[trnel]
runway	թռիչքուղի	[triʧku'hi]
visibility	տեսանելիություն	[tesaneliu'ʦyn]
flight (act of flying)	թռիչք	[triʧk]
altitude	բարձրություն	[barʣru'ʦyn]
air pocket	օդային փոս	[oda'jɪn 'pos]
seat	տեղ	[teh]
headphones	ականջակալներ	[akanʤakal'ner]
folding tray (tray table)	բացվող սեղանիկ	[baʦ'voh seha'nik]

airplane window	իլյումինատոր	[ilymi'nator]
aisle	անցուղի	[antsu'hi]

25. Train

train	գնացք	[gnatsk]
commuter train	էլեկտրագնացք	[ɛlektrag'natsk]
express train	արագընթաց գնացք	[aragɪn'tats g'natsk]
diesel locomotive	ջերմաքարշ	[ʤerma'karʃ]
steam locomotive	շոգեքարշ	[ʃoke'karʃ]
passenger car	վագոն	[va'gon]
dining car	վագոն-ռեստորան	[va'gon resto'ran]
rails	գծեր	[gtser]
railroad	երկաթգիծ	[erkat'gits]
railway tie	կոճ	[koʧ]
platform (railway ~)	կառամատույց	[karama'tujts]
track (~ 1, 2, etc.)	ուղի	[u'hi]
semaphore	նշանասյուն	[nʃʌna'syn]
station	կայարան	[kaja'ran]
engineer (train driver)	մեքենավար	[mekena'var]
porter (of luggage)	բեռնակիր	[berna'kir]
car attendant	ուղեկից	[uhe'kits]
passenger	ուղևոր	[uhe'vor]
conductor (ticket inspector)	հսկիչ	[ɛs'kiʧ]
corridor (in train)	միջանցք	[mi'ʤantsk]
emergency brake	ավտոմատ կանգառման սարք	[avto'mat kaŋar'man 'sark]
compartment	կուպե	[ku'pe]
berth	մահճակ	[mah'ʧak]
upper berth	վերևի մահճակատեղ	[vere'vi mahʧaka'teh]
lower berth	ներքևի մահճակատեղ	[nerke'vi mahʧaka'teh]
bed linen, bedding	անկողին	[aŋko'hin]
ticket	տոմս	[toms]
schedule	չվացուցակ	[ʧvatsu'tsak]
information display	ցուցատախտակ	[tsutsatah'tak]
to leave, to depart	մեկնել	[mek'nel]
departure (of train)	մեկնում	[mek'num]
to arrive (ab. train)	ժամանել	[ʒama'nel]
arrival	ժամանում	[ʒama'num]
to arrive by train	ժամանել գնացքով	[ʒama'nel gnats'kov]
to get on the train	գնացք նստել	[g'natsk nstel]

to get off the train	գնացքից իջնել	[gnatsʼkits idʒʼnel]
train wreck	խորտակում	[hortaʼkum]
steam locomotive	շոգեքարշ	[ʃokeʼkarʃ]
stoker, fireman	հնոցապան	[ɛnotsaʼpan]
firebox	վառարան	[varaʼran]
coal	ածուխ	[aʼtsuh]

26. Ship

ship	նավ	[nav]
vessel	նավ	[nav]
steamship	շոգենավ	[ʃogeʼnav]
riverboat	ջերմանավ	[dʒermaʼnav]
cruise ship	լայներ	[ʼlajner]
cruiser	հածանավ	[atsaʼnav]
yacht	զբոսանավ	[zbosaʼnav]
tugboat	նավաքարշ	[navaʼkarʃ]
barge	բեռնանավ	[bernaʼnav]
ferry	լաստանավ	[lastaʼnav]
sailing ship	առագաստանավ	[aragastaʼnav]
brigantine	բրիգանտինա	[briganʼtina]
ice breaker	սառցահատ	[sartsaʼnav]
submarine	սուզանավ	[suzaʼnav]
boat (flat-bottomed ~)	նավակ	[naʼvak]
dinghy	մակույկ	[maʼkujk]
lifeboat	փրկարարական մակույկ	[prkararaʼkan maʼkujk]
motorboat	մոտորանավակ	[motoranaʼvak]
captain	նավապետ	[navaʼpet]
seaman	նավաստի	[navasʼti]
sailor	ծովային	[tsovaʼjın]
crew	անձնակազմ	[andznaʼkazm]
boatswain	բոցման	[botsʼman]
ship's boy	նավի փոքրավոր	[naʼvi pokraʼvor]
cook	նավի խոհարար	[naʼvi hoaʼrar]
ship's doctor	նավի բժիշկ	[naʼvi bʼʒiʃk]
deck	տախտակամած	[tahtakaʼmats]
mast	կայմ	[kajm]
sail	առագաստ	[araʼgast]
hold	նավամբար	[navamʼbar]
bow (prow)	նավաքիթ	[navaʼkit]
stern	նավախել	[navaʼhel]

oar	թիակ	[ti'ak]
screw propeller	պտուտակ	[ptu'tak]
cabin	նավասենյակ	[navase'ɲak]
wardroom	ընդհանուր նավասենյակ	[ında'nur navase'ɲak]
engine room	մեքենաների բաժանմունք	[mekenane'ri baʒan'muŋk]
bridge	նավապետի կամրջակ	[navape'ti kamr'ʤak]
radio room	ռադիոխցիկ	[radioh'tsik]
wave (radio)	ալիք	[a'lik]
logbook	նավամատյան	[navama'tʲan]
spyglass	հեռադիտակ	[ɛradi'tak]
bell	զանգ	[zaŋ]
flag	դրոշ	[droʃ]
rope (mooring ~)	ճոպան	[ʧo'pan]
knot (bowline, etc.)	հանգույց	[a'ŋujʦ]
deckrails	բռնաձող	[brna'ʣoh]
gangway	նավասանդուղք	[navasan'duhk]
anchor	խարիսխ	[ha'rish]
to weigh anchor	խարիսխը բարձրացնել	[ha'rishı barʣraʦ'nel]
to drop anchor	խարիսխը գցել	[ha'rishı g'ʦel]
anchor chain	խարսխաշղթա	[harshaʃh'ta]
port (harbor)	նավահանգիստ	[nava:'ŋist]
quay, wharf	նավամատույց	[navama'tujʦ]
to berth (moor)	կառանել	[kara'nel]
to cast off	մեկնել	[mek'nel]
trip, voyage	ճանապարհորդություն	[ʧanaparordu'tsyn]
cruise (sea trip)	ծովագնացություն	[ʦovagnaʦu'tsyn]
course (route)	ուղղություն	[uhu'tsyn]
route (itinerary)	երթուղի	[ertu'hi]
fairway	նավարկուղի	[navarku'hi]
shallows	ծանծաղուտ	[ʦanʦa'hut]
to run aground	ծանծաղուտ ընկնել	[ʦanʦa'hut ıŋk'nel]
storm	փոթորիկ	[poto'rik]
signal	ազդանշան	[azdan'ʃʌn]
to sink (vi)	խորտակվել	[hortak'vel]
SOS (distress signal)	SOS	['sos]
ring buoy	փրկագոտի	[prkago'ti]

CITY

T&P Books Publishing

27. Urban transportation

bus	ավտոբուս	[avto'bus]
streetcar	տրամվայ	[tram'vaj]
trolley bus	տրոլեյբուս	[trolej'bus]
route (of bus, etc.)	ուղի	[u'hi]
number (e.g., bus ~)	համար	[a'mar]
to go by ...	... ով գնալ	[ov g'nal]
to get on (~ the bus)	նստել	[nstel]
to get off ...	իջնել	[idʒ'nel]
stop (e.g., bus ~)	կանգառ	[ka'ŋar]
next stop	հաջորդ կանգառ	[a'dʒord ka'ŋar]
terminus	վերջին կանգառ	[ver'dʒin ka'ŋar]
schedule	ժամանակացույց	[ʒamanaka'ʦujʦ]
to wait (vt)	սպասել	[spa'sel]
ticket	տոմս	[toms]
fare	տոմսի արժեքը	[tom'si ar'ʒekı]
cashier (ticket seller)	տոմսավաճառ	[tomsava'ʧar]
ticket inspection	ստուգում	[stu'gum]
ticket inspector	հսկիչ	[ɛs'kiʧ]
to be late (for ...)	ուշանալ	[uʃʌ'nal]
to miss (~ the train, etc.)	ուշանալ ... ից	[uʃʌ'nal 'iʦ]
to be in a hurry	շտապել	[ʃta'pel]
taxi, cab	տակսի	[tak'si]
taxi driver	տակսու վարորդ	[tak'su va'rord]
by taxi	տակսիով	[taksi'ov]
taxi stand	տակսիների կայան	[taksine'ri ka'jan]
to call a taxi	տակսի կանչել	[tak'si kan'ʧel]
to take a taxi	տակսի վերցնել	[tak'si verʦ'nel]
traffic	ճանապարհային երթևեկություն	[ʧanapara'jın erteveku'ʦyn]
traffic jam	խցանում	[hʦa'num]
rush hour	պիկ ժամ	['pik 'ʒam]
to park (vi)	կանգնեցնել	[kaŋeʦ'nel]
to park (vt)	կանգնեցնել	[kaŋeʦ'nel]
parking lot	ավտոկայան	[avtoka'jan]
subway	մետրո	[met'ro]
station	կայարան	[kaja'ran]

to take the subway	մետրոյով գնալ	[metro'jov g'nal]
train	գնացք	[gnatsk]
train station	կայարան	[kaja'ran]

28. City. Life in the city

city, town	քաղաք	[ka'hak]
capital city	մայրաքաղաք	[majraka'hak]
village	գյուղ	[gyh]
city map	քաղաքի հատակագիծ	[kaha'ki ataka'gits]
downtown	քաղաքի կենտրոն	[kaha'ki kent'ron]
suburb	արվարձան	[arvar'dzan]
suburban (adj)	մերձքաղաքային	[merdzkahaka'jɪn]
outskirts	ծայրամաս	[tsajra'mas]
environs (suburbs)	շրջակայք	[ʃrdʒa'kajk]
city block	թաղամաս	[taha'mas]
residential block (area)	բնակելի թաղամաս	[bnake'li taha'mas]
traffic	երթևեկություն	[erteveku'tsyn]
traffic lights	լուսակիր	[lusa'kir]
public transportation	քաղաքային տրանսպորտ	[kahaka'jɪn trans'port]
intersection	խաչմերուկ	[hatʃme'ruk]
crosswalk	անցում	[an'tsum]
pedestrian underpass	գետնանցում	[getnan'tsum]
to cross (~ the street)	անցնել	[ants'nel]
pedestrian	հետիոտն	[ɛti'otn]
sidewalk	մայթ	[majt]
bridge	կամուրջ	[ka'murdʒ]
embankment (river walk)	առափնյա փողոց	[arap'ɲa po'hots]
fountain	շատրվան	[ʃʌtr'van]
allée (garden walkway)	ծառուղի	[tsaru'hi]
park	զբոսայգի	[zbosaj'gi]
boulevard	բուլվար	[buʎ'var]
square	հրապարակ	[ɛrapa'rak]
avenue (wide street)	պողոտա	[po'hota]
street	փողոց	[po'hots]
side street	նրբանցք	[nrbantsk]
dead end	փակուղի	[paku'hi]
house	տուն	[tun]
building	շենք	[ʃəŋk]
skyscraper	երկնաքեր	[erkna'ker]
facade	ճակատամաս	[tʃakata'mas]
roof	տանիք	[ta'nik]

window	պատուհան	[patu'an]
arch	կամար	[ka'mar]
column	սյուն	[syn]
corner	անկյուն	[a'ŋkyn]
store window	ցուցափեղկ	[tsutsa'pehk]
signboard (store sign, etc.)	ցուցանակ	[tsutsa'nak]
poster	ազդագիր	[azda'gir]
advertising poster	գովազդային ձգապաստառ	[govazda'jɪn dzgapas'tar]
billboard	գովազդային վահանակ	[govazda'jɪn va:'nak]
garbage, trash	աղբ	[ahb]
trashcan (public ~)	աղբաման	[ahba'man]
to litter (vi)	աղբոտել	[ahbo'tel]
garbage dump	աղբավայր	[ahba'vajr]
phone booth	հեռախոսախցիկ	[ɛrahosah'tsik]
lamppost	լապտերասյուն	[laptera'syn]
bench (park ~)	նստարան	[nsta'ran]
police officer	ոստիկան	[vosti'kan]
police	ոստիկանություն	[vostikanu'tsyn]
beggar	մուրացկան	[murats'kan]
homeless (n)	անօթևան մարդ	[anote'van 'mard]

29. Urban institutions

store	խանութ	[ha'nut]
drugstore, pharmacy	դեղատուն	[deha'tun]
eyeglass store	օպտիկա	['optika]
shopping mall	առևտրի կենտրոն	[arevt'ri kent'ron]
supermarket	սուպերմարքեթ	[supermar'ket]
bakery	հացաբուլկեղենի խանութ	[atsabulkehe'ni ha'nut]
baker	հացթուխ	[ats'tuh]
candy store	հրուշակեղենի խանութ	[ɛruʃʌkehe'ni ha'nut]
grocery store	նպարեղենի խանութ	[nparehe'ni ha'nut]
butcher shop	մսի խանութ	[m'si ha'nut]
produce store	բանջարեղենի կրպակ	[bandʒarehe'ni kr'pak]
market	շուկա	[ʃu'ka]
coffee house	սրճարան	[srtʃa'ran]
restaurant	ռեստորան	[resto'ran]
pub, bar	գարեջրատուն	[garedʒra'tun]
pizzeria	պիցցերիա	[pitse'ria]
hair salon	վարսավիրանոց	[varsavira'nots]
post office	փոստ	[post]

dry cleaners	քիմմաքրման կետ	[kimmakr'man 'ket]
photo studio	ֆոտոսրահ	[fotos'rah]
shoe store	կոշիկի սրահ	[koʃi'ki s'rah]
bookstore	գրախանութ	[graha'nut]
sporting goods store	սպորտային խանութ	[sporta'jın ha'nut]
clothes repair shop	հագուստի վերանորոգում	[agus'ti veranoro'gum]
formal wear rental	հագուստի վարձույթ	[agus'ti var'dzujt]
video rental store	տեսաֆիլմերի վարձույթ	[tesafilme'ri var'dzujt]
circus	կրկես	[krkes]
zoo	կենդանաբանական այգի	[kendanabana'kan aj'gi]
movie theater	կինոթատրոն	[kinotat'ron]
museum	թանգարան	[taŋa'ran]
library	գրադարան	[grada'ran]
theater	թատրոն	[tat'ron]
opera (opera house)	օպերա	[ope'ra]
nightclub	գիշերային ակումբ	[giʃəra'jın a'kumb]
casino	խաղատուն	[haha'tun]
mosque	մզկիթ	[mzkit]
synagogue	սինագոգ	[sina'gog]
cathedral	տաճար	[ta'ʧar]
temple	տաճար	[ta'ʧar]
church	եկեղեցի	[ekehe'ʦi]
college	ինստիտուտ	[insti'tut]
university	համալսարան	[amalsa'ran]
school	դպրոց	[dproʦ]
prefecture	ոստիկանապետություն	[vostikanapetu'ʦyn]
city hall	քաղաքապետարան	[kahakapeta'ran]
hotel	հյուրանոց	[jura'noʦ]
bank	բանկ	[baŋk]
embassy	դեսպանատուն	[despana'tun]
travel agency	տուրիստական գործակալություն	[turista'kan gorʦakalu'ʦyn]
information office	տեղեկատվական բյուրո	[tehekatva'kan by'ro]
currency exchange	փոխանակման կետ	[pohanak'man 'ket]
subway	մետրո	[met'ro]
hospital	հիվանդանոց	[ivanda'noʦ]
gas station	բենզալցակայան	[benzalʦaka'jan]
parking lot	ավտոկայան	[avtoka'jan]

30. Signs

signboard (store sign, etc.)	ցուցանակ	[ʦuʦa'nak]
notice (door sign, etc.)	ցուցագիր	[ʦuʦa'gir]
poster	ձգապաստառ	[ʣgapas'tar]
direction sign	ուղեցույց	[uhe'ʦujʦ]
arrow (sign)	սլաք	[slak]
caution	նախազգուշացում	[nahazguʃʌ'ʦum]
warning sign	զգուշացում	[zguʃʌ'ʦum]
to warn (vt)	զգուշացնել	[zguʃʌʦ'nel]
rest day (weekly ~)	հանգստյան օր	[aŋs'tʲan 'or]
timetable (schedule)	ժամանակացույց	[ʒamanaka'ʦujʦ]
opening hours	աշխատանքային ժամեր	[aʃhataŋka'jɪn ʒa'mer]
WELCOME!	ԲԱՐԻ ԳԱԼՈ՛ՒՍՏ	[ba'ri ga'lust]
ENTRANCE	ՄՈՒՏՔ	[mutk]
EXIT	ԵԼՔ	[elk]
PUSH	ԴԵՊԻ ԴՈՒՐՍ	[de'pi 'durs]
PULL	ԴԵՊԻ ՆԵՐՍ	['depi 'ners]
OPEN	ԲԱՑ Է	[baʦ ɛ]
CLOSED	ՓԱԿ Է	[pak ɛ]
WOMEN	ԿԱՆԱՆՑ ՀԱՄԱՐ	[ka'nanʦ a'mar]
MEN	ՏՂԱՄԱՐԴԿԱՆՑ ՀԱՄԱՐ	[thamard'kanʦ a'mar]
DISCOUNTS	ԶԵՂՉԵՐ	[zeh'ʧer]
SALE	Ի ՍՊԱՌ ՎԱՃԱՌՔ	[i s'par va'ʧark]
NEW!	ՆՈՐՈ՛ՒՅԹ	[no'rujt]
FREE	ԱՆՎՃԱՐ	[anv'ʧar]
ATTENTION!	ՈՒՇԱԴՐՈՒԹՅՈ՛ՒՆ	[uʃʌdru'ʦyn]
NO VACANCIES	ՏԵՂԵՐ ՉԿԱՆ	[te'her ʧ'kan]
RESERVED	ՊԱՏՎԻՐՎԱԾ Է	[patvir'vaʦ ɛ]
ADMINISTRATION	ԱԴՄԻՆԻՍՏՐԱՑԻԱ	[administ'raʦia]
STAFF ONLY	ՄԻԱՅՆ ԱՇԽԱՏԱԿԻՑՆԵՐԻ ՀԱՄԱՐ	[mi'ajn aʃhatakiʦne'ri a'mar]
BEWARE OF THE DOG!	ԿԱՏԱՂԻ ՇՈՒՆ	[kata'hi 'ʃun]
NO SMOKING	Չ՛ԾԽԵԼ	[ʧʦ'hel]
DO NOT TOUCH!	ՁԵՌՔ ՉՏԱ՛Լ	[ʣerk ʧ'tal]
DANGEROUS	ՎՏԱՆԳԱՎՈՐ Է	[vtaŋa'vor ɛ]
DANGER	ՎՏԱՆԳԱՎՈՐ Է	[vtaŋa'vor ɛ]
HIGH VOLTAGE	ԲԱՐՁՐ ԼԱՐՈՒՄ	['barʣr la'rum]
NO SWIMMING!	ԼՈՂԱԼՆ ԱՐԳԵԼՎՈՒՄ Է	[lo'haln argel'vum ɛ]
OUT OF ORDER	ՉԻ ԱՇԽԱՏՈՒՄ	[ʧi aʃha'tum]

FLAMMABLE	ՀՐԱՎՏԱՆԳԱՎՈՐ Է	[ɛravtaŋa'vor ɛ]
FORBIDDEN	ԱՐԳԵԼՎԱԾ Է	[argel'vats ɛ]
NO TRESPASSING!	ԱՆՑՆԵԼՆ ԱՐԳԵԼՎԱԾ Է	[ants'neln argel'vats ɛ]
WET PAINT	ՆԵՐԿՎԱԾ Է	[nerk'vats ɛ]

31. Shopping

to buy (purchase)	գնել	[gnel]
purchase	գնում	[gnum]
to go shopping	գնումներ կատարել	[gnum'ner kata'rel]
shopping	գնումներ	[gnum'ner]
to be open (ab. store)	աշխատել	[aʃha'tel]
to be closed	փակվել	[pak'vel]
footwear, shoes	կոշիկ	[ko'ʃik]
clothes, clothing	հագուստ	[a'gust]
cosmetics	կոսմետիկա	[kos'metika]
food products	մթերքներ	[mterk'ner]
gift, present	նվեր	[nver]
salesman	վաճառող	[vatʃa'roh]
saleswoman	վաճառողուհի	[vatʃarohu'i]
check out, cash desk	դրամարկղ	[dra'markh]
mirror	հայելի	[aje'li]
counter (store ~)	վաճառասեղան	[vatʃarase'han]
fitting room	հանդերձարան	[anderdza'ran]
to try on	փորձել	[por'dzel]
to fit (ab. dress, etc.)	սազել	[sa'zel]
to like (I like ...)	դուր գալ	['dur gal]
price	գին	[gin]
price tag	գնապիտակ	[gnapi'tak]
to cost (vt)	արժենալ	[arʒe'nal]
How much?	Որքա՞ն արժե:	[vor'kan ar'ʒe]
discount	զեղչ	[zehtʃ]
inexpensive (adj)	ոչ թանկ	['votʃ taŋk]
cheap (adj)	էժան	[ɛ'ʒan]
expensive (adj)	թանկ	[taŋk]
It's expensive	Սա թանկ է:	[sa 'taŋk ɛ]
rental (n)	վարձույթ	[var'dzujt]
to rent (~ a tuxedo)	վարձել	[var'dzel]
credit (trade credit)	վարկ	[vark]
on credit (adv)	վարկով	[var'kov]

CLOTHING & ACCESSORIES

T&P Books Publishing

32. Outerwear. Coats

clothes	հագուստ	[a'gust]
outerwear	վերնազգեստ	[vernaz'gest]
winter clothing	ձմեռային հագուստ	[dzmera'jɪn a'gust]
coat (overcoat)	վերարկու	[verar'ku]
fur coat	մուշտակ	[muʃ'tak]
fur jacket	կիսամուշտակ	[kisamuʃ'tak]
down coat	բմբուլե բաճկոն	[bmbu'lɛ batʃ'kon]
jacket (e.g., leather ~)	բաճկոն	[batʃ'kon]
raincoat (trenchcoat, etc.)	թիկնոց	[tik'nots]
waterproof (adj)	անջրանցիկ	[andʒran'tsik]

33. Men's & women's clothing

shirt (button shirt)	վերնաշապիկ	[vernaʃʌ'pik]
pants	տաբատ	[ta'bat]
jeans	ջինսեր	[dʒin'ser]
suit jacket	պիջակ	[pi'dʒak]
suit	կոստյում	[kos'tym]
dress (frock)	զգեստ	[zgest]
skirt	շրջազգեստ	[ʃrdʒaz'gest]
blouse	բլուզ	[bluz]
knitted jacket (cardigan, etc.)	կոֆտա	[kof'ta]
jacket (of woman's suit)	ժակետ	[ʒa'ket]
T-shirt	մարզաշապիկ	[marzaʃʌ'pik]
shorts (short trousers)	կարճ տաբատ	['kartʃ ta'bat]
tracksuit	մարզազգեստ	[marzaz'gest]
bathrobe	խալաթ	[ha'lat]
pajamas	ննջազգեստ	[ŋdʒaz'gest]
sweater	սվիտեր	[svi'ter]
pullover	պուլովեր	[pu'lover]
vest	բաճկոնակ	[batʃko'nak]
tailcoat	ֆրակ	[frak]
tuxedo	սմոկինգ	[s'mokiŋ]
uniform	համազգեստ	[amaz'gest]
workwear	աշխատանքային համազգեստ	[aʃhataŋka'jɪn amaz'gest]

overalls	կոմբինեզոն	[kombine'zon]
coat (e.g., doctor's smock)	խալաթ	[ha'lat]

34. Clothing. Underwear

underwear	ներքնազգեստ	[nerknaz'gest]
undershirt (A-shirt)	ներքնաշապիկ	[nerknaʃʌ'pik]
socks	կիսագուլպա	[kisagul'pa]
nightgown	գիշերանոց	[giʃəra'nots]
bra	կրծքակալ	[krtskal]
knee highs (knee-high socks)	կարճ գուլպաներ	['kartʃ gulpa'ner]
pantyhose	զուգագուլպա	[zugagul'pa]
stockings (thigh highs)	գուլպաներ	[gulpa'ner]
bathing suit	լողազգեստ	[lohaz'gest]

35. Headwear

hat	գլխարկ	[glhark]
fedora	եզրավոր գլխարկ	[ezra'vor gl'hark]
baseball cap	մարզագլխարկ	[marzagl'hark]
flatcap	կեպի	['kepi]
beret	բերետ	[be'ret]
hood	գլխանոց	[glha'nots]
panama hat	պանամա	[pa'nama]
knit cap (knitted hat)	գործած գլխարկ	[gor'tsats gl'hark]
headscarf	գլխաշոր	[glha'ʃor]
women's hat	գլխարկիկ	[glhar'kik]
hard hat	սաղավարտ	[saha'vart]
garrison cap	պիլոտկա	[pi'lotka]
helmet	սաղավարտ	[saha'vart]
derby	կոտելոկ	[kote'lok]
top hat	գլանագլխարկ	[glanagl'hark]

36. Footwear

footwear	կոշիկ	[ko'ʃik]
shoes (men's shoes)	ճտքավոր կոշիկներ	[tʃtka'vor koʃik'ner]
shoes (women's shoes)	կոշիկներ	[koʃik'ner]
boots (cowboy ~)	երկարաճիտ կոշիկներ	[erkara'tʃit koʃik'ner]
slippers	հողաթափեր	[ohata'per]

tennis shoes (e.g., Nike ~)	բոթասներ	[botas'ner]
sneakers (e.g., Converse ~)	մարզական կոշիկներ	[marza'kan koʃik'ner]
sandals	սանդալներ	[sandal'ner]
cobbler (shoe repairer)	կոշկակար	[koʃka'kar]
heel	կրունկ	[kruŋk]
pair (of shoes)	զույգ	[zujg]
shoestring	կոշկակապ	[koʃka'kap]
to lace (vt)	կոշկակապել	[koʃkaka'pel]
shoehorn	թիակ	[ti'ak]
shoe polish	կոշիկի քսուք	[koʃi'ki k'suk]

37. Personal accessories

gloves	ձեռնոցներ	[ʣernoʦ'ner]
mittens	ձեռնոց	[ʣer'noʦ]
scarf (muffler)	շարֆ	[ʃʌrf]
glasses (eyeglasses)	ակնոց	[ak'noʦ]
frame (eyeglass ~)	շրջանակ	[ʃrʤa'nak]
umbrella	հովանոց	[ova'noʦ]
walking stick	ձեռնափայտ	[ʣerna'pajt]
hairbrush	մազերի խոզանակ	[maze'ri hoza'nak]
fan	հովհար	[o'var]
tie (necktie)	փողկապ	[poh'kap]
bow tie	փողկապ-թիթեռնիկ	[poh'kap titer'nik]
suspenders	տաբատակալ	[tabata'kal]
handkerchief	թաշկինակ	[taʃki'nak]
comb	սանր	[sanr]
barrette	մազակալ	[maza'kal]
hairpin	ծամկալ	[ʦam'kal]
buckle	ճարմանդ	[ʧar'mand]
belt	գոտի	[go'ti]
shoulder strap	փոկ	[pok]
bag (handbag)	պայուսակ	[paju'sak]
purse	կանացի պայուսակ	[kana'ʦi paju'sak]
backpack	ուղեպարկ	[uhe'park]

38. Clothing. Miscellaneous

fashion	նորաձևություն	[noraʣevu'ʦyn]
in vogue (adj)	նորաձև	[nora'ʣev]

fashion designer	մոդելյեր	[mode'ʎjer]
collar	օձիք	[o'dzik]
pocket	գրպան	[grpan]
pocket (as adj)	գրպանի	[grpa'ni]
sleeve	թևք	[tevk]
hanging loop	կախիչ	[ka'hitʃ]
fly (on trousers)	լայնույթ	[laj'nujt]
zipper (fastener)	կայծակաճարմանդ	[kajsaka tʃar'mand]
fastener	ճարմանդ	[tʃar'mand]
button	կոճակ	[ko'tʃak]
buttonhole	հանգույց	[a'ŋujts]
to come off (ab. button)	պոկվել	[pok'vel]
to sew (vi, vt)	կարել	[ka'rel]
to embroider (vi, vt)	ասեղնագործել	[asehnagor'tsel]
embroidery	ասեղնագործություն	[asehnagortsu'tsyn]
sewing needle	ասեղ	[a'seh]
thread	թել	[tel]
seam	կար	[kar]
to get dirty (vi)	կեղտոտվել	[kehtot'vel]
stain (mark, spot)	բիծ	[bits]
to crease, crumple (vi)	ճմրթվել	[tʃmrtel]
to tear, to rip (vt)	ճղվել	[tʃhvel]
clothes moth	ցեց	[tsets]

39. Personal care. Cosmetics

toothpaste	ատամի մածուկ	[ata'mi ma'tsuk]
toothbrush	ատամի խոզանակ	[ata'mi hoza'nak]
to brush one's teeth	ատամները մաքրել	[atam'nerı mak'rel]
razor	ածելի	[atse'li]
shaving cream	սափրվելու կրեմ	[saprve'lu k'rem]
to shave (vi)	սափրվել	[sapr'vel]
soap	օճառ	[o'tʃar]
shampoo	շամպուն	[ʃʌm'pun]
scissors	մկրատ	[mkrat]
nail file	խարտոց	[har'tots]
nail clippers	ունելիք	[une'lik]
tweezers	ունելի	[une'li]
cosmetics	կոսմետիկա	[kos'metika]
face mask	դիմակ	[di'mak]
manicure	մանիկյուր	[mani'kyr]
to have a manicure	մատնահարդարում	[matna:rda'rum]
pedicure	պեդիկյուր	[pedi'kyr]

make-up bag	կոսմետիկայի պայուսակ	[kosmetika'jı paju'sak]
face powder	դիմափոշի	[dimapo'ʃi]
powder compact	դիմափոշու աման	[dimapo'ʃu a'man]
blusher	կարմրաներկ	[karmra'nerk]
perfume (bottled)	օծանելիք	[otsane'lik]
toilet water (perfume)	անուշահոտ ջուր	[anuʃʌ'ot 'dʒur]
lotion	լոսյոն	[lo'sʲon]
cologne	օդեկոլոն	[odeko'lon]
eyeshadow	կոպերի ներկ	[kope'ri 'nerk]
eyeliner	աչքի մատիտ	[atʃ'ki ma'tit]
mascara	տուշ	[tuʃ]
lipstick	շրթներկ	[ʃrtnerk]
nail polish, enamel	եղունգների լաք	[ehuŋe'ri 'lak]
hair spray	մազերի լաք	[maze'ri 'lak]
deodorant	դեզոդորանտ	[dezodo'rant]
cream	կրեմ	[krem]
face cream	դեմքի կրեմ	[dem'ki k'rem]
hand cream	ձեռքի կրեմ	[dzer'ki k'rem]
anti-wrinkle cream	կնճիռների դեմ կրեմ	[kntʃirne'ri 'dem k'rem]
day (as adj)	ցերեկային	[tsereka'jın]
night (as adj)	գիշերային	[giʃəra'jın]
tampon	տամպոն	[tam'pon]
toilet paper	զուգարանի թուղթ	[zugara'ni 'tuht]
hair dryer	ֆեն	[fen]

40. Watches. Clocks

watch (wristwatch)	ձեռքի ժամացույց	[dzer'ki ʒama'tsujts]
dial	թվահարթակ	[tva:r'tak]
hand (of clock, watch)	սլաք	[slak]
metal watch band	շղթա	[ʃhta]
watch strap	փոկ	[pok]
battery	մարտկոց	[mart'kots]
to be dead (battery)	նստել	[nstel]
to change a battery	մարտկոցը փոխել	[mart'kotsı po'hel]
to run fast	առաջ ընկնել	[a'radʒ ıŋk'nel]
to run slow	ետ ընկնել	['et ıŋk'nel]
wall clock	պատի ժամացույց	[pa'ti ʒama'tsujts]
hourglass	ավազի ժամացույց	[ava'zi ʒama'tsujts]
sundial	արևի ժամացույց	[are'vi ʒama'tsujts]
alarm clock	զարթուցիչ	[zartu'tsitʃ]
watchmaker	ժամագործ	[ʒama'gorts]
to repair (vt)	նորոգել	[noro'gel]

EVERYDAY EXPERIENCE

T&P Books Publishing

41. Money

money	դրամ	[dram]
currency exchange	փոխանակում	[pohana'kum]
exchange rate	փոխարժեք	[pohar'ʒek]
ATM	բանկոմատ	[baŋko'mat]
coin	մետաղադրամ	[metahad'ram]
dollar	դոլլար	[dol'lar]
euro	եվրո	['evro]
lira	լիրա	['lira]
Deutschmark	մարկ	[mark]
franc	ֆրանկ	[fraŋk]
pound sterling	ֆունտ ստերլինգ	['funt s'terliŋ]
yen	յեն	[jen]
debt	պարտք	[partk]
debtor	պարտապան	[parta'pan]
to lend (money)	պարտքով տալ	[part'kov 'tal]
to borrow (vi, vt)	պարտքով վերցնել	[part'kov verts'nel]
bank	բանկ	[baŋk]
account	հաշիվ	[a'ʃiv]
to deposit into the account	հաշվի վրա գցել	[aʃ'vi vra g'tsel]
to withdraw (vt)	հաշվից հանել	[aʃ'vits a'nel]
credit card	վարկային քարտ	[varka'jɪn 'kart]
cash	կանխիկ դրամ	[kan'hik d'ram]
check	չեք	[tʃek]
to write a check	չեք դուրս գրել	[tʃek durs g'rel]
checkbook	չեքային գրքույկ	[tʃeka'jɪn gr'kujk]
wallet	թղթապանակ	[thtapa'nak]
change purse	դրամապանակ	[dramapa'nak]
billfold	դրամապանակ	[dramapa'nak]
safe	չհրկիզվող պահարան	[tʃrkiz'voh pa:'ran]
heir	ժառանգ	[ʒa'raŋ]
inheritance	ժառանգություն	[ʒaraŋu'tsyn]
fortune (wealth)	ունեցվածք	[unets'vatsk]
lease	վարձ	[vardz]
rent (money)	բնակվարձ	[bnak'vardz]
to rent (sth from sb)	վարձել	[var'dzel]
price	գին	[gin]

cost	արժեք	[ar'ʒek]
sum	գումար	[gu'mar]
to spend (vt)	ծախսել	[ʦah'sel]
expenses	ծախսեր	[ʦah'ser]
to economize (vi, vt)	տնտեսել	[tnte'sel]
economical	տնտեսող	[tnte'soh]
to pay (vi, vt)	վճարել	[vʧa'rel]
payment	վճար	[v'ʧar]
change (give the ~)	մանր	[manr]
tax	հարկ	[ark]
fine	տուգանք	[tu'gaŋk]
to fine (vt)	տուգանել	[tuga'nel]

42. Post. Postal service

post office	փոստ	[post]
mail (letters, etc.)	փոստ	[post]
mailman	փոստատար	[posta'tar]
opening hours	աշխատանքային ժամեր	[aʃhataŋka'jɪn ʒa'mer]
letter	նամակ	[na'mak]
registered letter	պատվիրված նամակ	[patvir'vaʦ na'mak]
postcard	բացիկ	[ba'ʦik]
telegram	հեռագիր	[ɛra'gir]
package (parcel)	ծանրոց	[ʦan'roʦ]
money transfer	դրամային փոխանցում	[drama'jɪn pohan'ʦum]
to receive (vt)	ստանալ	[sta'nal]
to send (vt)	ուղարկել	[uhar'kel]
sending	ուղարկում	[uhar'kum]
address	հասցե	[as'ʦe]
ZIP code	ինդեքս	[in'deks]
sender	ուղարկող	[uhar'koh]
receiver	ստացող	[sta'ʦoh]
name (first name)	անուն	[a'nun]
surname (last name)	ազգանուն	[azga'nun]
postage rate	սակագին	[saka'gin]
standard (adj)	սովորական	[sovora'kan]
economical (adj)	տնտեսող	[tnte'soh]
weight	քաշ	[kaʃ]
to weigh (~ letters)	կշռել	[kʃrel]
envelope	ծրար	[ʦrar]
postage stamp	նամականիշ	[namaka'niʃ]

43. Banking

bank	բանկ	[baŋk]
branch (of bank, etc.)	բաժանմունք	[baʒan'muŋk]
bank clerk, consultant	խորհրդատու	[horɛrda'tu]
manager (director)	կառավարիչ	[karava'ritʃ]
bank account	հաշիվ	[a'ʃiv]
account number	հաշվի համար	[aʃ'vi a'mar]
checking account	ընթացիկ հաշիվ	[ɛnta'tsik a'ʃiv]
savings account	կուտակային հաշիվ	[kutaka'jɪn a'ʃiv]
to open an account	հաշիվ բացել	[a'ʃiv ba'tsel]
to close the account	հաշիվ փակել	[a'ʃiv pa'kel]
to deposit into the account	հաշվի վրա գցել	[aʃ'vi vra g'tsel]
to withdraw (vt)	հաշվից հանել	[aʃ'vits a'nel]
deposit	ավանդ	[a'vand]
to make a deposit	ավանդ ներդնել	[a'vand nerd'nel]
wire transfer	փոխանցում	[pohan'tsum]
to wire, to transfer	փոխանցում կատարել	[pohan'tsum kata'rel]
sum	գումար	[gu'mar]
How much?	Որքա՞ն	[vor'kan]
signature	ստորագրություն	[storagru'tsyn]
to sign (vt)	ստորագրել	[storag'rel]
credit card	վարկային քարտ	[varka'jɪn 'kart]
code (PIN code)	կոդ	[kod]
credit card number	վարկային քարտի համար	[varka'jɪn kar'ti a'mar]
ATM	բանկոմատ	[baŋko'mat]
check	չեք	[tʃek]
to write a check	չեք դուրս գրել	[tʃek durs g'rel]
checkbook	չեքային գրքույկ	[tʃeka'jɪn gr'kujk]
loan (bank ~)	վարկ	[vark]
to apply for a loan	դիմել վարկ ստանալու համար	[di'mel 'vark stana'lu a'mar]
to get a loan	վարկ վերցնել	['vark verts'nel]
to give a loan	վարկ տրամադրել	['vark tramad'rel]
guarantee	գրավական	[grava'kan]

44. Telephone. Phone conversation

telephone	հեռախոս	[ɛra'hos]
mobile phone	բջջային հեռախոս	[bdʒa'jɪn ɛra'hos]

answering machine	ինքնապատասխանիչ	[iŋknapatasha'nitʃ]
to call (by phone)	զանգահարել	[zaŋa:'rel]
phone call	զանգ	[zaŋ]
to dial a number	համարը հավաքել	[a'marı ava'kel]
Hello!	Ալո՛	[a'lo]
to ask (vt)	հարցնել	[arʦ'nel]
to answer (vi, vt)	պատասխանել	[patasha'nel]
to hear (vt)	լսել	[lsel]
well (adv)	լավ	[lav]
not well (adv)	վատ	[vat]
noises (interference)	խանգարումներ	[haŋarum'ner]
receiver	լսափող	[lsa'poh]
to pick up (~ the phone)	լսափողը վերցնել	[lsa'pohı verʦ'nel]
to hang up (~ the phone)	լսափողը դնել	[lsa'pohı d'nel]
busy (adj)	զբաղված	[zbah'vaʦ]
to ring (ab. phone)	զանգել	[za'ŋel]
telephone book	հեռախոսագիրք	[ɛrahosa'girk]
local (adj)	տեղային	[teha'jın]
long distance (~ call)	միջքաղաքային	[miʤkahaka'jın]
international (adj)	միջազգային	[miʤazga'jın]

45. Mobile telephone

mobile phone	բջջային հեռախոս	[bʤa'jın ɛra'hos]
display	էկրան	[ɛk'ran]
button	կոճակ	[ko'ʧak]
SIM card	SIM-քարտ	[sim 'kart]
battery	մարտկոց	[mart'koʦ]
to be dead (battery)	լիցքաթափվել	[liʦkatap'vel]
charger	լիցքավորման սարք	[liʦkavor'man 'sark]
menu	մենյու	[me'ny]
settings	լարք	[lark]
tune (melody)	մեղեդի	[mehe'di]
to select (vt)	ընտրել	[ınt'rel]
calculator	հաշվիչ	[aʃ'viʧ]
voice mail	ինքնապատասխանիչ	[iŋknapatasha'niʧ]
alarm clock	զարթուցիչ	[zartu'ʦiʧ]
contacts	հեռախոսագիրք	[ɛrahosa'girk]
SMS (text message)	SMS-հաղորդագրություն	[SMS ahordagru'ʦyn]
subscriber	բաժանորդ	[baʒa'nord]

46. Stationery

ballpoint pen	ինքնահոս գրիչ	[iŋkna'os g'ritʃ]
fountain pen	փետրավոր գրիչ	[petra'vor g'ritʃ]
pencil	մատիտ	[ma'tit]
highlighter	նշիչ	[nʃitʃ]
felt-tip pen	ֆլոմաստեր	[flomas'ter]
notepad	նոթատետր	[nota'tetr]
agenda (diary)	օրագիրք	[ora'girg]
ruler	քանոն	[ka'non]
calculator	հաշվիչ	[aʃ'vitʃ]
eraser	ռետին	[re'tin]
thumbtack	սնեռակ	[seve'rak]
paper clip	ամրակ	[am'rak]
glue	սոսինձ	[so'sindz]
stapler	ճարմանդակարիչ	[tʃarmandaka'ritʃ]
hole punch	ծակոտիչ	[tsako'titʃ]
pencil sharpener	սրիչ	[sritʃ]

47. Foreign languages

language	լեզու	[le'zu]
foreign language	օտար լեզու	[o'tar le'zu]
to study (vt)	ուսումնասիրել	[usumnasi'rel]
to learn (language, etc.)	սովորել	[sovo'rel]
to read (vi, vt)	կարդալ	[kar'dal]
to speak (vi, vt)	խոսել	[ho'sel]
to understand (vt)	հասկանալ	[aska'nal]
to write (vt)	գրել	[grel]
fast (adv)	արագ	[a'rag]
slowly (adv)	դանդաղ	[dan'dah]
fluently (adv)	ազատ	[a'zat]
rules	կանոն	[ka'non]
grammar	քերականություն	[kerakanu'tsyn]
vocabulary	բառագիտություն	[baragitu'tsyn]
phonetics	հնչյունաբանություն	[ɛntʃunabanu'tsyn]
textbook	դասագիրք	[dasa'girk]
dictionary	բառարան	[bara'ran]
teach-yourself book	ինքնուսույց	[iŋknu'sujts]
phrasebook	զրուցարան	[zrutsa'ran]
cassette	ձայներիզ	[dzajne'riz]

videotape	տեսաերիզ	[tesae'riz]
CD, compact disc	խտասկավառակ	[htaskava'rak]
DVD	DVD-սկավառակ	[divi'di skava'rak]
alphabet	այբուբեն	[ajbu'ben]
to spell (vt)	տառերով արտասանել	[tare'rov artasa'nel]
pronunciation	արտասանություն	[artasanu'tsyn]
accent	ակցենտ	[ak'tsent]
with an accent	ակցենտով	[aktsen'tov]
without an accent	առանց ակցենտ	[a'rants ak'tsent]
word	բառ	[bar]
meaning	իմաստ	[i'mast]
course (e.g., a French ~)	դասընթաց	[dasɪn'tats]
to sign up	գրանցվել	[grants'vel]
teacher	ուսուցիչ	[usu'tsitʃ]
translation (process)	թարգմանություն	[targmanu'tsyn]
translation (text, etc.)	թարգմանություն	[targmanu'tsyn]
translator	թարգմանիչ	[targma'nitʃ]
interpreter	թարգմանիչ	[targma'nitʃ]
polyglot	պոլիգլոտ	[polig'lot]
memory	հիշողություն	[iʃohu'tsyn]

MEALS. RESTAURANT

T&P Books Publishing

48. Table setting

spoon	գդալ	[gdal]
knife	դանակ	[da'nak]
fork	պատառաքաղ	[patara'kah]
cup (e.g., coffee ~)	բաժակ	[ba'ʒak]
plate (dinner ~)	ափսե	[ap'se]
saucer	պնակ	[pnak]
napkin (on table)	անձեռոցիկ	[andzero'tsik]
toothpick	ատամնափորիչ	[atamnapo'ritʃ]

49. Restaurant

restaurant	ռեստորան	[resto'ran]
coffee house	սրճարան	[srtʃa'ran]
pub, bar	բար	[bar]
tearoom	թեյարան	[teja'ran]
waiter	մատուցող	[matu'tsoh]
waitress	մատուցողուհի	[matutsohu'i]
bartender	բարմեն	[bar'men]
menu	մենյու	[me'ny]
wine list	գինիների գրացանկ	[ginine'ri gra'tsaŋk]
to book a table	սեղան պատվիրել	[se'han patvi'rel]
course, dish	ուտեստ	[u'test]
to order (meal)	պատվիրել	[patvi'rel]
to make an order	պատվեր կատարել	[pat'ver kata'rel]
aperitif	ապերիտիվ	[aperi'tiv]
appetizer	խորտիկ	[hor'tik]
dessert	աղանդեր	[ahan'der]
check	հաշիվ	[a'ʃiv]
to pay the check	հաշիվը փակել	[a'ʃivɪ pa'kel]
to give change	մանրը վերադարձնել	['manrɪ veradarts'nel]
tip	թեյափող	[teja'poh]

50. Meals

food	կերակուր	[kera'kur]
to eat (vi, vt)	ուտել	[u'tel]

breakfast	նախաճաշ	[naha'ʧaʃ]
to have breakfast	նախաճաշել	[nahaʧa'ʃəl]
lunch	ճաշ	[ʧaʃ]
to have lunch	ճաշել	[ʧa'ʃəl]
dinner	ընթրիք	[ɪnt'rik]
to have dinner	ընթրել	[ɪnt'rel]
appetite	ախորժակ	[ahor'ʒak]
Enjoy your meal!	Բարի՛ ախորժակ:	[ba'ri ahor'ʒak]
to open (~ a bottle)	բացել	[ba'ʦel]
to spill (liquid)	թափել	[ta'pel]
to spill out (vi)	թափվել	[tap'vel]
to boil (vi)	եռալ	[e'ral]
to boil (vt)	եռացնել	[eraʦ'nel]
boiled (~ water)	եռացրած	[eraʦ'raʦ]
to chill, cool down (vt)	սառեցնել	[sareʦ'nel]
to chill (vi)	սառեցվել	[sareʦ'vel]
taste, flavor	համ	[am]
aftertaste	կողմնակի համ	[kohmna'ki 'am]
to slim down (lose weight)	նիհարել	[nia'rel]
diet	սննդակարգ	[sŋda'karg]
vitamin	վիտամին	[vita'min]
calorie	կալորիա	[ka'lorija]
vegetarian (n)	բուսակեր	[busa'ker]
vegetarian (adj)	բուսակերական	[busakera'kan]
fats (nutrient)	ճարպեր	[ʧar'per]
proteins	սպիտակուցներ	[spitakuʦ'ner]
carbohydrates	ածխաջրեր	[aʦhaʤ'rer]
slice (of lemon, ham)	պատառ	[pa'tar]
piece (of cake, pie)	կտոր	[ktor]
crumb (of bread, cake, etc.)	փշուր	[pʃur]

51. Cooked dishes

course, dish	ճաշատեսակ	[ʧaʃʌte'sak]
cuisine	խոհանոց	[hoa'noʦ]
recipe	բաղադրատոմս	[bahadra'toms]
portion	բաժին	[ba'ʒin]
salad	աղցան	[ah'ʦan]
soup	ապուր	[a'pur]
clear soup (broth)	մսաջուր	[msa'ʤur]
sandwich (bread)	բրդուճ	[brduʧ]

fried eggs	ձվածեղ	[dzva'tseh]
fried meatballs	կոտլետ	[kot'let]
hamburger (beefburger)	համբուրգեր	[ambur'ger]
beefsteak	բիֆշտեքս	[biffʃ'teks]
stew	տապակած միս	[tapa'kats 'mis]
side dish	գառնիր	[gar'nir]
spaghetti	սպագետի	[spa'getti]
mashed potatoes	կարտոֆիլի պյուրե	[kartofi'li py're]
pizza	պիցցա	['pitsa]
porridge (oatmeal, etc.)	շիլա	[ʃi'la]
omelet	ձվածեղ	[dzva'tseh]
boiled (e.g., ~ beef)	եփած	[e'pats]
smoked (adj)	ապխտած	[aph'tats]
fried (adj)	տապակած	[tapa'kats]
dried (adj)	չորացրած	[tʃorats'rats]
frozen (adj)	սառեցված	[sarets'vats]
pickled (adj)	մարինացված	[marinats'vats]
sweet (sugary)	քաղցր	[kahtsr]
salty (adj)	աղի	[a'hi]
cold (adj)	սառը	['sarı]
hot (adj)	տաք	[tak]
bitter (adj)	դառը	['darı]
tasty (adj)	համեղ	[a'meh]
to cook in boiling water	եփել	[e'pel]
to cook (dinner)	պատրաստել	[patras'tel]
to fry (vt)	տապակել	[tapa'kel]
to heat up (food)	տաքացնել	[takats'nel]
to salt (vt)	աղ անել	['ah a'nel]
to pepper (vt)	պղպեղ անել	[ph'peh a'nel]
to grate (vt)	քերել	[ke'rel]
peel (n)	կլեպ	[klep]
to peel (vt)	կլպել	[klpel]

52. Food

meat	միս	[mis]
chicken	հավ	[av]
Rock Cornish hen (poussin)	ճուտ	[tʃut]
duck	բադ	[bad]
goose	սագ	[sag]
game	որսամիս	[vorsa'mis]
turkey	հնդկահավ	[ındka'av]
pork	խոզի միս	[ho'zi 'mis]
veal	հորթի միս	[or'ti 'mis]

lamb	ոչխարի միս	[votʃha'ri 'mis]
beef	տավարի միս	[tava'ri 'mis]
rabbit	ճագար	[tʃa'gar]
sausage (bologna, pepperoni, etc.)	երշիկ	[er'ʃik]
vienna sausage (frankfurter)	նրբերշիկ	[nrber'ʃik]
bacon	բեկոն	[be'kon]
ham	խոզապուխտ	[hoza'puht]
gammon	ազդր	[azdr]
pâté	պաշտետ	[paʃ'tet]
liver	լյարդ	[ʎard]
lard	սալ	[sal]
hamburger (ground beef)	աղացած միս	[aha'tsats 'mis]
tongue	լեզու	[le'zu]
egg	ձու	[dzu]
eggs	ձվեր	[dzver]
egg white	սպիտակուց	[spita'kuts]
egg yolk	դեղնուց	[deh'nuts]
fish	ձուկ	[dzuk]
seafood	ծովամթերքներ	[tsovamterk'ner]
caviar	ձկնկիթ	[dzkŋkit]
crab	ծովախեցգետին	[tsovahetsge'tin]
shrimp	մանր ծովախեցգետին	['manr tsovahetsge'tin]
oyster	ոստրե	[vost're]
spiny lobster	լանգուստ	[la'ŋust]
octopus	ութոտնուկ	[utvot'nuk]
squid	կաղամար	[kaha'mar]
sturgeon	թառափ	[ta'rap]
salmon	սաղման	[sah'man]
halibut	վահանաձուկ	[va:na'dzuk]
cod	ձողաձուկ	[dzoha'dzuk]
mackerel	թյունիկ	[ty'nik]
tuna	թյունոս	[ty'ŋos]
eel	օձաձուկ	[odza'dzuk]
trout	իշխան	[iʃ'han]
sardine	սարդինա	[sar'dina]
pike	գայլաձուկ	[gajla'dzuk]
herring	ծովատառեխ	[tsovata'reh]
bread	հաց	[hats]
cheese	պանիր	[pa'nir]
sugar	շաքար	[ʃʌ'kar]
salt	աղ	[ah]

rice	բրինձ	[brinʤ]
pasta	մակարոն	[maka'ron]
noodles	լափշա	[lap'ʃʌ]
butter	սերուցքային կարագ	[serutska'jɪn ka'rag]
vegetable oil	բուսական յուղ	[busa'kan 'juh]
sunflower oil	արևածաղկի ձեթ	[arevatsah'ki 'ʤet]
margarine	մարգարին	[marga'rin]
olives	ձիթապտուղ	[ʤitap'tuh]
olive oil	ձիթապտղի ձեթ	[ʤitapt'hi 'ʤet]
milk	կաթ	[kat]
condensed milk	խտացրած կաթ	[htats'rats 'kat]
yogurt	յոգուրտ	[jo'gurt]
sour cream	թթվասեր	[ttva'ser]
cream (of milk)	սերուցք	[se'rutsk]
mayonnaise	մայոնեզ	[majo'nez]
buttercream	կրեմ	[krem]
cereal grains (wheat, etc.)	ձավար	[ʤa'var]
flour	ալյուր	[a'lyr]
canned food	պահածոներ	[pa:tso'ner]
cornflakes	եգիպտացորենի փաթիլներ	[egiptatsore'ni patil'ner]
honey	մեղր	[mehr]
jam	ջեմ	[ʤem]
chewing gum	մաստակ	[mas'tak]

53. Drinks

water	ջուր	[ʤur]
drinking water	խմելու ջուր	[hme'lu 'ʤur]
mineral water	հանքային ջուր	[aŋka'jɪn 'ʤur]
still (adj)	առանց գազի	[a'rants ga'zi]
carbonated (adj)	գազավորված	[gazavor'vats]
sparkling (adj)	գազով	[ga'zov]
ice	սառույց	[sa'rujts]
with ice	սառույցով	[saru'tsov]
non-alcoholic (adj)	ոչ ալկոհոլային	['voʧ alko:la'jɪn]
soft drink	ոչ ալկոհոլային ըմպելիք	['voʧ alko:la'jɪn ɪmpe'lik]
refreshing drink	զովացուցիչ ըմպելիք	[zovatsu'tsiʧ ɪmpe'lik]
lemonade	լիմոնադ	[limo'nad]
liquors	ալկոհոլային խմիչքներ	[alko:la'jɪn hmiʧk'ner]
wine	գինի	[gi'ni]

white wine	սպիտակ գինի	[spi'tak gi'ni]
red wine	կարմիր գինի	[kar'mir gi'ni]
liqueur	լիկյոր	[li'k3r]
champagne	շամպայն	[ʃʌm'pajn]
vermouth	վերմուտ	['vermut]
whisky	վիսկի	['viski]
vodka	օղի	[o'hi]
gin	ջին	[ʤin]
cognac	կոնյակ	[ko'ɲjak]
rum	ռոմ	[rom]
coffee	սուրճ	[surʧ]
black coffee	սև սուրճ	[sev 'surʧ]
coffee with milk	կաթով սուրճ	[ka'tov 'surʧ]
cappuccino	սերուցքով սուրճ	[seruʦ'kov 'surʧ]
instant coffee	լուծվող սուրճ	[luʦ'voh 'surʧ]
milk	կաթ	[kat]
cocktail	կոկտեյլ	[kok'tejʎ]
milkshake	կաթնային կոկտեյլ	[katna'jɪn kok'tejʎ]
juice	հյութ	[hjut]
tomato juice	տոմատի հյութ	[toma'ti h'jut]
orange juice	նարնջի հյութ	[narn'ʤi h'jut]
freshly squeezed juice	թարմ քամված հյութ	['tarm kam'vaʦ h'jut]
beer	գարեջուր	[gare'ʤur]
light beer	բաց գարեջուր	['baʦ gare'ʤur]
dark beer	մուգ գարեջուր	['mug gare'ʤur]
tea	թեյ	[tej]
black tea	սև թեյ	[sev 'tej]
green tea	կանաչ թեյ	[ka'naʧ 'tej]

54. Vegetables

vegetables	բանջարեղեն	[banʤare'hen]
greens	կանաչի	[kana'ʧi]
tomato	լոլիկ	[lo'lik]
cucumber	վարունգ	[va'ruŋ]
carrot	գազար	[ga'zar]
potato	կարտոֆիլ	[karto'fil]
onion	սոխ	[soh]
garlic	սխտոր	[shtor]
cabbage	կաղամբ	[ka'hamb]
cauliflower	ծաղկակաղամբ	[ʦahkaka'hamb]

Brussels sprouts	բրյուսելյան կաղամբ	[bryse'ʎan ka'hamb]
broccoli	կաղամբ բրոկոլի	[ka'hamb bro'koli]
beetroot	բազուկ	[ba'zuk]
eggplant	սմբուկ	[smbuk]
zucchini	դդմիկ	[ddmik]
pumpkin	դդում	[ddum]
turnip	շաղգամ	[ʃʌh'gam]
parsley	մաղադանոս	[mahada'nos]
dill	սամիթ	[sa'mit]
lettuce	սալաթ	[sa'lat]
celery	նեխուր	[ne'hur]
asparagus	ծնեբեկ	[ʦne'bek]
spinach	սպինատ	[spi'nat]
pea	սիսեռ	[si'ser]
beans	լոբի	[lo'bi]
corn (maize)	եգիպտացորեն	[egiptaʦo'ren]
kidney bean	լոբի	[lo'bi]
bell pepper	պղպեղ	[phpeh]
radish	բողկ	[bohk]
artichoke	արտիճուկ	[arti'ʧuk]

55. Fruits. Nuts

fruit	միրգ	[mirg]
apple	խնձոր	[hnʣor]
pear	տանձ	[tanʣ]
lemon	կիտրոն	[kit'ron]
orange	նարինջ	[na'rinʤ]
strawberry	ելակ	[e'lak]
mandarin	մանդարին	[manda'rin]
plum	սալոր	[sa'lor]
peach	դեղձ	[dehʣ]
apricot	ծիրան	[ʦi'ran]
raspberry	մորի	[mo'ri]
pineapple	արքայախնձոր	[arkajahn'ʣor]
banana	բանան	[ba'nan]
watermelon	ձմերուկ	[ʣme'ruk]
grape	խաղող	[ha'hoh]
sour cherry	բալ	[bal]
sweet cherry	կեռաս	[ke'ras]
melon	սեխ	[seh]
grapefruit	գրեյպֆրուտ	[grejpf'rut]
avocado	ավոկադո	[avo'kado]

papaya	պապայա	[pa'paja]
mango	մանգո	['maŋo]
pomegranate	նուռ	[nur]
redcurrant	կարմիր հաղարջ	[kar'mir a'hardʒ]
blackcurrant	սև հաղարջ	['sev a'hardʒ]
gooseberry	հաղարջ	[a'hardʒ]
bilberry	հապալաս	[apa'las]
blackberry	մոշ	[moʃ]
raisin	չամիչ	[tʃa'mitʃ]
fig	թուզ	[tuz]
date	արմավ	[ar'mav]
peanut	գետնընկույզ	[getnɪ'ŋkujz]
almond	նուշ	[nuʃ]
walnut	ընկույզ	[ɪ'ŋkujz]
hazelnut	պնդուկ	[pnduk]
coconut	կոկոսի ընկույզ	[ko'kosi ɪ'ŋkujz]
pistachios	պիստակ	[pis'tak]

56. Bread. Candy

bakers' confectionery (pastry)	հրուշակեղեն	[ɛruʃʌke'hen]
bread	հաց	[hats]
cookies	թխվածքաբլիթ	[thvatskab'lit]
chocolate (n)	շոկոլադ	[ʃoko'lad]
chocolate (as adj)	շոկոլադե	[ʃokola'dɛ]
candy	կոնֆետ	[kon'fet]
cake (e.g., cupcake)	հրուշակ	[ɛru'ʃʌk]
cake (e.g., birthday ~)	տորթ	[tort]
pie (e.g., apple ~)	կարկանդակ	[karkan'dak]
filling (for cake, pie)	լցոն	[ltson]
whole fruit jam	մուրաբա	[mura'ba]
marmalade	մարմելադ	[marme'lad]
waffles	վաֆլի	[vaf'li]
ice-cream	պաղպաղակ	[pahpa'hak]

57. Spices

salt	աղ	[ah]
salty (adj)	աղի	[a'hi]
to salt (vt)	աղ անել	['ah a'nel]
black pepper	սև պղպեղ	[sev ph'peh]

red pepper (milled ~)	կարմիր պղպեղ	[kar'mir ph'peh]
mustard	մանանեխ	[mana'neh]
horseradish	ծովաբողկ	[ʦova'bohk]
condiment	համեմունք	[ame'muŋk]
spice	համեմունք	[ame'muŋk]
sauce	սոուս	[so'us]
vinegar	քացախ	[ka'ʦah]
anise	անիսոն	[ani'son]
basil	ռեհան	[re'han]
cloves	մեխակ	[me'hak]
ginger	իմբիր	[im'birʲ]
coriander	գինձ	[gindz]
cinnamon	դարչին	[dar'ʧin]
sesame	քնջութ	[knʤut]
bay leaf	դափնու տերև	[dap'nu te'rev]
paprika	պապրիկա	['paprika]
caraway	չաման	[ʧa'man]
saffron	շաֆրան	[ʃʌf'ran]

PERSONAL INFORMATION. FAMILY

T&P Books Publishing

58. Personal information. Forms

name (first name)	անուն	[a'nun]
surname (last name)	ազգանուն	[azga'nun]
date of birth	ծննդյան ամսաթիվ	[tsŋ'dʲan amsa'tiv]
place of birth	ծննդավայր	[tsŋda'vajr]
nationality	ազգություն	[azgu'tsyn]
place of residence	բնակության վայրը	[bnaku'tsʲan 'vajrı]
country	երկիր	[er'kir]
profession (occupation)	մասնագիտություն	[masnagi'tsyn]
gender, sex	սեռ	[ser]
height	հասակ	[a'sak]
weight	քաշ	[kaʃ]

59. Family members. Relatives

mother	մայր	[majr]
father	հայր	[ajr]
son	որդի	[vor'di]
daughter	դուստր	[dustr]
younger daughter	կրտսեր դուստր	[kr'tser 'dustr]
younger son	կրտսեր որդի	[kr'tser vor'di]
eldest daughter	ավագ դուստր	[a'vag 'dustr]
eldest son	ավագ որդի	[a'vag vor'di]
brother	եղբայր	[eh'bajr]
sister	քույր	[kujr]
mom, mommy	մայրիկ	[maj'rik]
dad, daddy	հայրիկ	[aj'rik]
parents	ծնողներ	[tsnoh'ner]
child	երեխա	[ere'ha]
children	երեխաներ	[ereha'ner]
grandmother	տատիկ	[ta'tik]
grandfather	պապիկ	[pa'pik]
grandson	թոռ	[tor]
granddaughter	թոռնուհի	[tornu'i]
grandchildren	թոռներ	[tor'ner]
nephew	քրոջորդի, քրոջ աղջիկ	[krodʒor'di], [k'rodʒ ah'dʒik]
niece	եղբորորդի, եղբոր աղջիկ	[ehboror'di, eh'bor ah'dʒik]

mother-in-law (wife's mother)	**զոքանչ**	[zo'kanʧ]
father-in-law (husband's father)	**սկեսրայր**	[skes'rajr]
son-in-law (daughter's husband)	**փեսա**	[pe'sa]
stepmother	**խորթ մայր**	[hort 'majr]
stepfather	**խորթ հայր**	[hort 'ajr]
infant	**ծծկեր երեխա**	[ʦ'ker ere'ha]
baby (infant)	**մանուկ**	[ma'nuk]
little boy, kid	**պստիկ**	[pstik]
wife	**կին**	[kin]
husband	**ամուսին**	[amu'sin]
spouse (husband)	**ամուսին**	[amu'sin]
spouse (wife)	**կին**	[kin]
married (masc.)	**ամուսնացած**	[amusna'ʦaʦ]
married (fem.)	**ամուսնացած**	[amusna'ʦaʦ]
single (unmarried)	**ամուրի**	[amu'ri]
bachelor	**ամուրի**	[amu'ri]
divorced (masc.)	**ամուսնալուծված**	[amusnaluʦ'vaʦ]
widow	**այրի կին**	[aj'ri 'kin]
widower	**այրի տղամարդ**	[aj'ri tha'mard]
relative	**ազգական**	[azga'kan]
close relative	**մերձավոր ազգական**	[merʣa'vor azga'kan]
distant relative	**հեռավոր ազգական**	[ɛra'vor azga'kan]
relatives	**հարազատներ**	[arazat'ner]
orphan (boy or girl)	**որբ**	[vorb]
guardian (of minor)	**խնամակալ**	[hnama'kal]
to adopt (a boy)	**որդեգրել**	[vordeg'rel]
to adopt (a girl)	**որդեգրել**	[vordeg'rel]

60. Friends. Coworkers

friend (masc.)	**ընկեր**	[ɪ'ŋker]
friend (fem.)	**ընկերուհի**	[ɪŋkeru'i]
friendship	**ընկերություն**	[ɪŋkeru'ʦyn]
to be friends	**ընկերություն անել**	[ɪŋkeru'ʦyn a'nel]
buddy (masc.)	**բարեկամ**	[bare'kam]
buddy (fem.)	**բարեկամուհի**	[barekamu'i]
partner	**գործընկեր**	[gorʦɪ'ŋker]
chief (boss)	**շեֆ**	[ʃəf]
superior (n)	**պետ**	[pet]
subordinate (n)	**ենթակա**	[enta'ka]

colleague	**գործընկեր**	[gortsɪ'ŋker]
acquaintance (person)	**ծանոթ**	[tsa'not]
fellow traveler	**ուղեկից**	[uhe'kits]
classmate	**համադասարանցի**	[amadasaran'tsi]
neighbor (masc.)	**հարևան**	[are'van]
neighbor (fem.)	**հարևանուհի**	[arevanu'i]
neighbors	**հարևաններ**	[areva'ŋer]

HUMAN BODY. MEDICINE

T&P Books Publishing

61. Head

head	գլուխ	[gluh]
face	երես	[e'res]
nose	քիթ	[kit]
mouth	բերան	[be'ran]
eye	աչք	[atʃk]
eyes	աչքեր	[atʃ'ker]
pupil	բիբ	[bib]
eyebrow	ունք	[uŋk]
eyelash	թարթիչ	[tar'titʃ]
eyelid	կոպ	[kap]
tongue	լեզու	[le'zu]
tooth	ատամ	[a'tam]
lips	շրթունքներ	[ʃrtuŋk'ner]
cheekbones	այտոսկրեր	[ajtosk'rer]
gum	լինդ	[lind]
palate	քիմք	[kimk]
nostrils	քթածակեր	[ktatsa'ker]
chin	կզակ	[kzak]
jaw	ծնոտ	[tsnot]
cheek	այտ	[ajt]
forehead	ճակատ	[tʃa'kat]
temple	քներակ	[kne'rak]
ear	ականջ	[a'kandʒ]
back of the head	ծոծրակ	[tsots'rak]
neck	պարանոց	[para'nots]
throat	կոկորդ	[ko'kord]
hair	մազեր	[ma'zer]
hairstyle	սանրվածք	[sanr'vatsk]
haircut	սանրվածք	[sanr'vatsk]
wig	կեղծամ	[keh'tsam]
mustache	բեղեր	[be'her]
beard	մորուք	[mo'ruk]
to have (a beard, etc.)	կրել	[krel]
braid	հյուս	[hjus]
sideburns	այտամորուք	[ajtamo'ruk]
red-haired (adj)	շիկահեր	[ʃika'ɛr]
gray (hair)	ալեհեր	[ale'ɛr]

bald (adj)	ճաղատ	[ʧa'hat]
bald patch	ճաղատ	[ʧa'hat]
ponytail	պոչ	[poʧ]
bangs	մազափունջ	[maza'punʤ]

62. Human body

hand	դաստակ	[das'tak]
arm	թև	[tev]
finger	մատ	[mat]
thumb	բութ մատ	[but 'mat]
little finger	ճկույթ	[ʧkujt]
nail	եղունգ	[e'huŋ]
fist	բռունցք	[bruntsk]
palm	ափ	[ap]
wrist	դաստակ	[das'tak]
forearm	նախաբազուկ	[nahaba'zuk]
elbow	արմունկ	[ar'muŋk]
shoulder	ուս	[us]
leg	ոտք	[votk]
foot	ոտնաթաթ	[votna'tat]
knee	ծունկ	[tsuŋk]
calf (part of leg)	սրունք	[sruŋk]
hip	ազդր	[azdr]
heel	կրունկ	[kruŋk]
body	մարմին	[mar'min]
stomach	փոր	[por]
chest	կրծքավանդակ	[krtskavan'dak]
breast	կուրծք	[kurtsk]
flank	կող	[koh]
back	մեջք	[meʤk]
lower back	գոտկատեղ	[gotka'teh]
waist	գոտկատեղ	[gotka'teh]
navel (belly button)	պորտ	[port]
buttocks	նստատեղ	[nsta'teh]
bottom	հետույք	[ɛ'tujk]
beauty mark	խալ	[hal]
tattoo	դաջվածք	[daʤ'vatsk]
scar	սպի	[spi]

63. Diseases

sickness	հիվանդություն	[ivandu'tsyn]
to be sick	հիվանդ լինել	[i'vand li'nel]
health	առողջություն	[arohdʒu'tsyn]
runny nose (coryza)	հարբուխ	[ar'buh]
tonsillitis	անգինա	[a'ŋina]
cold (illness)	մրսածություն	[mrsatsu'tsyn]
to catch a cold	մրսել	[mrsel]
bronchitis	բրոնխիտ	[bron'hit]
pneumonia	թոքերի բորբոքում	[toke'ri borbo'kum]
flu, influenza	գրիպ	[grip]
nearsighted (adj)	կարճատես	[kartʃa'tes]
farsighted (adj)	հեռատես	[ɛra'hos]
strabismus (crossed eyes)	շլություն	[ʃlu'tsyn]
cross-eyed (adj)	շլաչք	[ʃlatʃk]
cataract	կատարակտա	[kata'rakta]
glaucoma	գլաուկոմա	[glau'koma]
stroke	ուղեղի կաթված	[uhe'hi kat'vats]
heart attack	ինֆարկտ	[in'farkt]
myocardial infarction	սրտամկանի կաթված	[srtamka'ni kat'vats]
paralysis	կաթված	[kat'vats]
to paralyze (vt)	կաթվածել	[katva'tsel]
allergy	ալերգիա	[aler'gia]
asthma	ասթմա	[ast'ma]
diabetes	շաքարախտ	[ʃʌka'raht]
toothache	ատամնացավ	[atamna'tsav]
caries	կարիես	[ka'ries]
diarrhea	լույծ	[lujts]
constipation	փորկապություն	[porkapu'tsyn]
stomach upset	ստամոքսի խանգարում	[stamok'si haŋa'rum]
food poisoning	թունավորում	[tunavo'rum]
to get food poisoning	թունավորվել	[tunavor'vel]
arthritis	հոդի բորբոքում	[o'di borbo'kum]
rickets	ռախիտ	[ra'hit]
rheumatism	հոդացավ	[oda'tsav]
atherosclerosis	աթերոսկլերոզ	[ateroskle'roz]
gastritis	գաստրիտ	[gast'rit]
appendicitis	ապենդիցիտ	[apendi'tsit]
cholecystitis	խոլեցիստիտ	[holetsis'tit]
ulcer	խոց	[hots]
measles	կարմրուկ	[karm'ruk]

rubella (German measles)	կարմրախտ	[karm'raht]
jaundice	դեղնախ	[deh'naht]
hepatitis	հեպատիտ	[ɛpa'tit]
schizophrenia	շիզոֆրենիա	[ʃizofre'nia]
rabies (hydrophobia)	կատաղություն	[katahu'tsyn]
neurosis	նեվրոզ	[nev'roz]
concussion	ուղեղի ցնցում	[uhe'hi tsn'tsum]
cancer	քաղծկեղ	[kahts'keh]
sclerosis	կարծրախտ	[karts'raht]
multiple sclerosis	ցրված կարծրախտ	[tsr'vats karts'raht]
alcoholism	հարբեցողություն	[arbetsohu'tsyn]
alcoholic (n)	հարբեցող	[arbe'tsoh]
syphilis	սիֆիլիս	[sifi'lis]
AIDS	ՁԻԱՀ	[dzi'ah]
tumor	ուռուցք	[u'rutsk]
malignant (adj)	չարորակ	[ʧaro'rak]
benign (adj)	բարորակ	[baro'rak]
fever	տենդ	[tend]
malaria	մալարիա	[mala'ria]
gangrene	փտախտ	[ptaht]
seasickness	ծովային հիվանդություն	[tsova'jɪn ivandu'tsyn]
epilepsy	ընկնավորություն	[ɛŋknavoru'tsyn]
epidemic	համաճարակ	[amaʧa'rak]
typhus	տիֆ	[tif]
tuberculosis	պալարախտ	[pala'raht]
cholera	խոլերա	[ho'lera]
plague (bubonic ~)	ժանտախտ	[ʒan'taht]

64. Symptoms. Treatments. Part 1

symptom	նախանշան	[nahan'ʃʌn]
temperature	ջերմաստիճան	[ʤermasti'ʧan]
high temperature (fever)	բարձր ջերմաստիճան	['bardzr ʤermasti'ʧan]
pulse	զարկերակ	[zarke'rak]
dizziness (vertigo)	գլխապտույտ	[glhap'tujt]
hot (adj)	տաք	[tak]
shivering	դողէրոցք	[dohɛ'rotsk]
pale (e.g., ~ face)	գունատ	[gu'nat]
cough	հազ	[az]
to cough (vi)	հազալ	[a'zal]
to sneeze (vi)	փռշտալ	[prʃtal]
faint	ուշագնացություն	[uʃʌgnatsu'tsyn]

to faint (vi)	ուշագնաց լինել	[uʃʌg'nats li'nel]
bruise (hématome)	կապտուկ	[kap'tuk]
bump (lump)	ուռուցք	[u'rutsk]
to bang (bump)	խփվել	[hpvel]
contusion (bruise)	վնասվածք	[vnas'vatsk]
to get a bruise	վնասվածք ստանալ	[vnas'vatsk sta'nal]
to limp (vi)	կաղալ	[ka'hal]
dislocation	հոդախախտում	[odahah'tum]
to dislocate (vt)	հոդախախտել	[odahah'tel]
fracture	կոտրվածք	[kotr'vatsk]
to have a fracture	կոտրվածք ստանալ	[kotr'vatsk sta'nal]
cut (e.g., paper ~)	կտրված վերք	[ktrvats 'verk]
to cut oneself	կտրել	[ktrel]
bleeding	արյունահոսություն	[arynaosu'tsyn]
burn (injury)	այրվածք	[ajr'vatsk]
to get burned	այրվել	[ajr'vel]
to prick (vt)	ծակել	[tsa'kel]
to prick oneself	ծակել	[tsa'kel]
to injure (vt)	վնասել	[vna'sel]
injury	վնասվածք	[vnas'vatsk]
wound	վերք	[verk]
trauma	վնասվածք	[vnas'vatsk]
to be delirious	զառանցել	[zaran'tsel]
to stutter (vi)	կակազել	[kaka'zel]
sunstroke	արևահարություն	[areva:ru'tsyn]

65. Symptoms. Treatments. Part 2

pain	ցավ	[tsav]
splinter (in foot, etc.)	փուշ	[puʃ]
sweat (perspiration)	քրտինք	[krtiŋk]
to sweat (perspire)	քրտնել	[krtnel]
vomiting	փսխում	[pshum]
convulsions	ջղաձգություն	[dʒhadzgu'tsyn]
pregnant (adj)	հղի	[ɛ'hi]
to be born	ծնվել	[tsnvel]
delivery, labor	ծննդաբերություն	[tsŋdaberu'tsyn]
to deliver (~ a baby)	ծննդաբերել	[tsŋdabe'rel]
abortion	աբորտ	[a'bort]
breathing, respiration	շնչառություն	[ʃntʃaru'tsyn]
in-breath (inhalation)	ներշնչում	[nerʃn'tʃum]
out-breath (exhalation)	արտաշնչում	[artaʃn'tʃum]

to exhale (breathe out)	արտաշնչել	[artaʃn'ʧel]
to inhale (vi)	շնչել	[ʃnʧel]
disabled person	հաշմանդամ	[aʃman'dam]
cripple	խեղանդամ	[hehan'dam]
drug addict	թմրամոլ	[tmra'mol]
deaf (adj)	խուլ	[hul]
mute (adj)	համր	[amr]
deaf mute (adj)	խուլ ու համր	['hul u 'amr]
mad, insane (adj)	խենթ	[hent]
to go insane	խենթանալ	[henta'nal]
gene	գեն	[gen]
immunity	իմունիտետ	[imuni'tet]
hereditary (adj)	ժառանգական	[ʒaraŋa'kan]
congenital (adj)	բնածին	[bna'ʦin]
virus	վարակ	[va'rak]
microbe	մանրէ	[man'rɛ]
bacterium	բակտերիա	[bak'teria]
infection	վարակ	[va'rak]

66. Symptoms. Treatments. Part 3

hospital	հիվանդանոց	[ivanda'noʦ]
patient	հիվանդ	[i'vand]
diagnosis	ախտորոշում	[ahtoro'ʃum]
cure	կազդուրում	[kazdu'rum]
medical treatment	բուժում	[bu'ʒum]
to get treatment	բուժվել	[buʒ'vel]
to treat (~ a patient)	բուժել	[bu'ʒel]
to nurse (look after)	խնամել	[hna'mel]
care (nursing ~)	խնամք	[hnamk]
operation, surgery	վիրահատություն	[vira:tu'ʦyn]
to bandage (head, limb)	վիրակապել	[viraka'pel]
bandaging	վիրակապում	[viraka'pum]
vaccination	պատվաստում	[patvas'tum]
to vaccinate (vt)	պատվաստում անել	[patvas'tum a'nel]
injection, shot	ներարկում	[nerar'kum]
to give an injection	ներարկել	[nerar'kel]
attack	նոպա	['nopa]
amputation	անդամահատություն	[andama:tu'ʦyn]
to amputate (vt)	անդամահատել	[andama:'tel]
coma	կոմա	['koma]

to be in a coma	կոմայի մեջ գտնվել	[koma'jı 'medʒ ıŋk'nel]
intensive care	վերակենդանացում	[verakendana'tsum]
to recover (~ from flu)	ապաքինվել	[apakin'vel]
condition (patient's ~)	վիճակ	[vi'tʃak]
consciousness	գիտակցություն	[gitaktsu'tsyn]
memory (faculty)	հիշողություն	[iʃohu'tsyn]
to pull out (tooth)	հեռացնել	[ɛrats'nel]
filling	պլոմբ	[plomb]
to fill (a tooth)	ատամը լցնել	[a'tamɛ lts'nel]
hypnosis	հիպնոս	[ip'nos]
to hypnotize (vt)	հիպնոսացնել	[ipnosats'nel]

67. Medicine. Drugs. Accessories

medicine, drug	դեղ	[deh]
remedy	դեղամիջոց	[dehami'dʒots]
to prescribe (vt)	դուրս գրել	['durs g'rel]
prescription	դեղատոմս	[deha'toms]
tablet, pill	հաբ	[ab]
ointment	քսուք	[ksuk]
ampule	ամպուլ	[am'pul]
mixture	հեղուկ դեղախառնուրդ	[ɛ'huk dehahar'nurd]
syrup	օշարակ	[oʃʌ'rak]
pill	հաբ	[ab]
powder	փոշի	[po'ʃi]
gauze bandage	վիրակապ ժապավեն	[vira'kap ʒapa'ven]
cotton wool	բամբակ	[bam'bak]
iodine	յոդ	[jod]
Band-Aid	սպեղանի	[speha'ni]
eyedropper	պիպետկա	[pi'petka]
thermometer	ջերմաչափ	[dʒerma'tʃap]
syringe	ներարկիչ	[nerar'kitʃ]
wheelchair	սայլակ	[saj'lak]
crutches	հենակներ	[ɛnak'ner]
painkiller	ցավազրկող	[tsavazr'koh]
laxative	լուծողական	[lutsoha'kan]
spirits (ethanol)	սպիրտ	[spirt]
medicinal herbs	խոտաբույս	[hota'bujs]
herbal (~ tea)	խոտաբուսային	[hotabusa'jın]

APARTMENT

T&P Books Publishing

68. Apartment

apartment	բնակարան	[bnaka'ran]
room	սենյակ	[se'ɲak]
bedroom	ննջարան	[ŋʤa'ran]
dining room	ճաշասենյակ	[ʧaʃʌse'ɲak]
living room	հյուրասենյակ	[jurase'ɲak]
study (home office)	աշխատասենյակ	[aʃhatase'ɲak]
entry room	նախասենյակ	[nahase'ɲak]
bathroom (room with a bath or shower)	լոգարան	[loga'ran]
half bath	զուգարան	[zuga'ran]
ceiling	առաստաղ	[aras'tah]
floor	հատակ	[a'tak]
corner	անկյուն	[a'ŋkyn]

69. Furniture. Interior

furniture	կահույք	[ka'ujk]
table	սեղան	[se'han]
chair	աթոռ	[a'tor]
bed	մահճակալ	[mahʧa'kal]
couch, sofa	բազմոց	[baz'mots]
armchair	բազկաթոռ	[bazka'tor]
bookcase	գրապահարան	[grapa:'ran]
shelf	դարակ	[da'rak]
shelving unit	գրադարակ	[grada'rak]
wardrobe	պահարան	[pa:'ran]
coat rack (wall-mounted ~)	կախարան	[kaha'ran]
coat stand	կախոց	[ka'hots]
bureau, dresser	կոմոդ	[ko'mod]
coffee table	սեղանիկ	[seha'nik]
mirror	հայելի	[aje'li]
carpet	գորգ	[gorg]
rug, small carpet	փոքր գորգ	[pokr 'gorg]
fireplace	բուխարի	[buha'ri]
candle	մոմ	[mom]

candlestick	մոմակալ	[moma'kal]
drapes	վարագույր	[vara'gujr]
wallpaper	պաստառ	[pas'tar]
blinds (jalousie)	շերտավարագույր	[ʃərtavara'gujr]
table lamp	սեղանի լամպ	[seha'ni 'lamp]
wall lamp (sconce)	ջահ	[dʒah]
floor lamp	ձողաջահ	[dzoha'dʒah]
chandelier	ջահ	[dʒah]
leg (of chair, table)	տոտիկ	[to'tik]
armrest	արմնկակալ	[armŋka'kal]
back (backrest)	թիկնակ	[tik'nak]
drawer	դարակ	[da'rak]

70. Bedding

bedclothes	սպիտակեղեն	[spitake'hen]
pillow	բարձ	[bardz]
pillowcase	բարձի երես	[bar'dzi e'res]
duvet, comforter	վերմակ	[ver'mak]
sheet	սավան	[sa'van]
bedspread	ծածկոց	[tsats'kots]

71. Kitchen

kitchen	խոհանոց	[hoa'nots]
gas	գազ	[gaz]
gas stove (range)	գազօջախ	[gazo'dʒah]
electric stove	էլեկտրական սալօջախ	[ɛlektra'kan salo'dʒah]
oven	ջեռոց	[dʒe'rots]
microwave oven	միկրոալիքային վառարան	[mikroalika'jɪn vara'ran]
refrigerator	սառնարան	[sarna'ran]
freezer	սառնախցիկ	[sarnah'tsik]
dishwasher	աման լվացող մեքենա	[a'man lva'tsoh meke'na]
meat grinder	մսաղաց	[msa'hats]
juicer	հյութաքամիչ	[jutaka'mitʃ]
toaster	տոստեր	[tos'ter]
mixer	հարիչ	[a'ritʃ]
coffee machine	սրճեփ	[srtʃep]
coffee pot	սրճաման	[srtʃa'man]
coffee grinder	սրճաղաց	[srtʃa'hats]
kettle	թեյնիկ	[tej'nik]
teapot	թեյաման	[teja'man]

lid	կափարիչ	[kapa'ritʃ]
tea strainer	թեյքամիչ	[tejka'mitʃ]
spoon	գդալ	[gdal]
teaspoon	թեյի գդալ	[tejı g'dal]
soup spoon	ճաշի գդալ	[tʃaʃi g'dal]
fork	պատառաքաղ	[patara'kah]
knife	դանակ	[da'nak]
tableware (dishes)	սպասք	[spask]
plate (dinner ~)	ափսե	[ap'se]
saucer	պնակ	[pnak]
shot glass	ըմպանակ	[ɛmpa'nak]
glass (tumbler)	բաժակ	[ba'ʒak]
cup	բաժակ	[ba'ʒak]
sugar bowl	շաքարաման	[ʃʌkara'man]
salt shaker	աղաման	[aha'man]
pepper shaker	պղպեղաման	[phpeha'man]
butter dish	կարագի աման	[kara'gi a'man]
stock pot (soup pot)	կաթսա	[ka'tsa]
frying pan (skillet)	թավա	[ta'va]
ladle	շերեփ	[ʃə'rep]
colander	քամիչ	[ka'mitʃ]
tray (serving ~)	սկուտեղ	[sku'teh]
bottle	շիշ	[ʃiʃ]
jar (glass)	բանկա	[ba'ŋka]
can	տարա	[ta'ra]
bottle opener	բացիչ	[ba'tsitʃ]
can opener	բացիչ	[ba'tsitʃ]
corkscrew	խցանահան	[htsana'an]
filter	զտիչ	[ztitʃ]
to filter (vt)	զտել	[ztel]
trash, garbage (food waste, etc.)	աղբ	[ahb]
trash can (kitchen ~)	աղբի դույլ	[ahbi 'dujl]

72. Bathroom

bathroom	լոգարան	[loga'ran]
water	ջուր	[dʒur]
faucet	ծորակ	[tso'rak]
hot water	տաք ջուր	[tak 'dʒur]
cold water	սառը ջուր	['sarı 'dʒur]
toothpaste	ատամի մածուկ	[ata'mi ma'tsuk]

to brush one's teeth	ատամները մաքրել	[atam'nerı mak'rel]
to shave (vi)	սափրվել	[sapr'vel]
shaving foam	սափրվելու փրփուր	[saprve'lu pr'pur]
razor	ածելի	[atse'li]
to wash (one's hands, etc.)	լվանալ	[lva'nal]
to take a bath	լվացվել	[lvats'vel]
shower	ցնցուղ	[tsntsuh]
to take a shower	դուշ ընդունել	['duʃ ındu'nel]
bathtub	լոգարան	[loha'ran]
toilet (toilet bowl)	զուգարանակոնք	[zugarana'koŋk]
sink (washbasin)	լվացարան	[lvatsa'ran]
soap	օճառ	[o'ʧar]
soap dish	օճառաման	[oʧara'man]
sponge	սպունգ	[spuŋ]
shampoo	շամպուն	[ʃʌm'pun]
towel	սրբիչ	[srbiʧ]
bathrobe	խալաթ	[ha'lat]
laundry (process)	լվացք	[lvatsk]
washing machine	լվացքի մեքենա	[lvats'ki meke'na]
to do the laundry	սպիտակեղեն լվալ	[spitake'hen l'val]
laundry detergent	լվացքի փոշի	[lvats'ki po'ʃi]

73. Household appliances

TV set	հեռուստացույց	[ɛrusta'tsujts]
tape recorder	մագնիտոֆոն	[magnito'fon]
VCR (video recorder)	տեսամագնիտոֆոն	[tesamagnito'fon]
radio	ընդունիչ	[ındu'niʧ]
player (CD, MP3, etc.)	նվագարկիչ	[nvagar'kiʧ]
video projector	տեսապրոյեկտոր	[tesaproek'tor]
home movie theater	տնային կինոթատրոն	[tna'jın kinotat'ron]
DVD player	DVD նվագարկիչ	[divi'di nvagar'kiʧ]
amplifier	ուժեղացուցիչ	[uʒehatsu'tsiʧ]
video game console	խաղային համակարգիչ	[haha'jın amakar'giʧ]
video camera	տեսախցիկ	[tesah'tsik]
camera (photo)	լուսանկարչական ապարատ	[lusaŋkarʧa'kan apa'rat]
digital camera	թվային լուսանկարչական ապարատ	[tva'jın lusaŋkarʧa'kan apa'rat]
vacuum cleaner	փոշեկուլ	[poʃə'kul]
iron (e.g., steam ~)	արդուկ	[ar'duk]
ironing board	արդուկի տախտակ	[ardu'ki tah'tak]

telephone	**հեռախոս**	[ɛra'hos]
mobile phone	**բջջային հեռախոս**	[bʤa'jɪn ɛra'hos]
typewriter	**տպող մեքենա**	[t'poh meke'na]
sewing machine	**կարի մեքենա**	[ka'ri meke'na]
microphone	**միկրոֆոն**	[mikro'fon]
headphones	**ականջակալներ**	[akanʤakal'ner]
remote control (TV)	**հեռակառավարման վահանակ**	[ɛrakaravar'man va:'nak]
CD, compact disc	**խտասկավառակ**	[htaskava'rak]
cassette	**ձայներիզ**	[ʣajne'riz]
vinyl record	**սկավառակ**	[skava'rak]

THE EARTH. WEATHER

T&P Books Publishing

74. Outer space

space	տիեզերք	[tie'zerk]
space (as adj)	տիեզերական	[tiezera'kan]
outer space	տիեզերական տարածություն	[tiezera'kan taratsu'tsyn]
world	աշխարհ	[aʃ'har]
universe	տիեզերք	[tie'zerk]
galaxy	գալակտիկա	[ga'laktika]
star	աստղ	[asth]
constellation	համաստեղություն	[amastehu'tsyn]
planet	մոլորակ	[molo'rak]
satellite	արբանյակ	[arba'ɲak]
meteorite	երկնաքար	[erkna'kar]
comet	գիսաստղ	[gi'sasth]
asteroid	աստղակերպ	[astha'kerp]
orbit	ուղեծիր	[uhe'tsir]
to revolve (~ around the Earth)	պտտվել	[ptɪt'vel]
atmosphere	մթնոլորտ	[mtno'lort]
the Sun	արեգակ	[are'gak]
solar system	արեգակնային համակարգ	[aregakna'jɪn ama'karg]
solar eclipse	արևի խավարում	[are'vi hava'rum]
the Earth	Երկիր	[er'kir]
the Moon	Լուսին	[lu'sin]
Mars	Մարս	[mars]
Venus	Վեներա	[ve'nera]
Jupiter	Յուպիտեր	[ju'piter]
Saturn	Սատուրն	[sa'turn]
Mercury	Մերկուրի	[mer'kuri]
Uranus	Ուրան	[u'ran]
Neptune	Նեպտուն	[nep'tun]
Pluto	Պլուտոն	[plu'ton]
Milky Way	Կաթնածիր	[katna'tsir]
Great Bear (Ursa Major)	Մեծ Արջ	[mets 'ardʒ]
North Star	Բևեռային Աստղ	[bevera'jɪn 'asth]
Martian	Մարսի բնակիչ	[mar'si bna'kitʃ]

extraterrestrial (n)	այլմոլորակային	[ajlmoloraka'jɪn]
alien	եկվոր	[ek'vor]
flying saucer	թռչող ափսե	[tr'ʧoh ap'se]
spaceship	տիեզերանավ	[tiezerag'naʦ]
space station	ուղեծրային կայան	[uheʦra'jɪn ka'jan]
blast-off	մեկնարկ	[meknat'riʧk]
engine	շարժիչ	[ʃʌr'ʒiʧ]
nozzle	փողելք	[po'helk]
fuel	վառելիք	[vare'lik]
cockpit, flight deck	խցիկ	[hʦik]
antenna	ալեհավաք	[alea'vak]
porthole	իլյումինատոր	[ilymi'nator]
solar panel	արևային մարտկոց	[areva'jɪn mart'koʦ]
spacesuit	սկաֆանդր	[ska'fandr]
weightlessness	անկշռություն	[aŋkʃru'ʦyn]
oxygen	թթվածին	[ttva'ʦin]
docking (in space)	միակցում	[miak'ʦum]
to dock (vi, vt)	միակցում կատարել	[miak'ʦum kata'rel]
observatory	աստղադիտարան	[asthadita'ran]
telescope	աստղադիտակ	[asthadi'tak]
to observe (vt)	հետևել	[ɛte'vel]
to explore (vt)	հետազոտել	[ɛtazo'tel]

75. The Earth

the Earth	Երկիր	[er'kir]
the globe (the Earth)	երկրագունդ	[erkra'gund]
planet	մոլորակ	[molo'rak]
atmosphere	մթնոլորտ	[mtno'lort]
geography	աշխարհագրություն	[aʃharagru'ʦyn]
nature	բնություն	[bnu'ʦyn]
globe (table ~)	գլոբուս	[glo'bus]
map	քարտեզ	[kar'tez]
atlas	ատլաս	[at'las]
Europe	Եվրոպա	[ev'ropa]
Asia	Ասիա	['asia]
Africa	Աֆրիկա	['afrika]
Australia	Ավստրալիա	[avst'ralia]
America	Ամերիկա	[a'merika]
North America	Հյուսիսային Ամերիկա	[jusisa'jɪn a'merika]

South America	Հարավային Ամերիկա	[arava'jın a'merika]
Antarctica	Անտարկտիդա	[antark'tida]
the Arctic	Արկտիկա	['arktika]

76. Cardinal directions

north	հյուսիս	[ju'sis]
to the north	դեպի հյուսիս	[de'pi ju'sis]
in the north	հյուսիսում	[jusi'sum]
northern (adj)	հյուսիսային	[jusisa'jın]
south	հարավ	[a'rav]
to the south	դեպի հարավ	[de'pi a'rav]
in the south	հարավում	[ara'vum]
southern (adj)	հարավային	[arava'jın]
west	արևմուտք	[arev'mutk]
to the west	դեպի արևմուտք	[de'pi arev'mutk]
in the west	արևմուտքում	[arevmut'kum]
western (adj)	արևմտյան	[arevm'tʲan]
east	արևելք	[are'velk]
to the east	դեպի արևելք	[de'pi are'velk]
in the east	արևելքում	[arevel'kum]
eastern (adj)	արևելյան	[areve'ʎan]

77. Sea. Ocean

sea	ծով	[ʦov]
ocean	օվկիանոս	[ovkia'nos]
gulf (bay)	ծոց	[ʦoʦ]
straits	նեղուց	[ne'huʦ]
land (solid ground)	ցամաք	[ʦa'mak]
continent (mainland)	մայրցամաք	[majrʦa'mak]
island	կղզի	[khzi]
peninsula	թերակղզի	[terakh'zi]
archipelago	արշիպելագ	[arʃipe'lag]
bay, cove	ծովախորշ	[ʦova'horʃ]
harbor	նավահանգիստ	[nava:'ŋist]
lagoon	ծովալճակ	[ʦoval'ʧak]
cape	հրվանդան	[ɛrvan'dan]
atoll	ատոլ	[a'tol]
reef	խութ	[hut]
coral	մարջան	[mar'ʤan]
coral reef	մարջանախութ	[marʤana'hut]

deep (adj)	**խորը**	['horı]
depth (deep water)	**խորություն**	[horu'ʦyn]
abyss	**անդունդ**	[an'dund]
trench (e.g., Mariana ~)	**ծովախորշ**	[ʦova'horʃ]
current (Ocean ~)	**հոսանք**	[o'saŋk]
to surround (bathe)	**ողողել**	[voho'hel]
shore	**ափ**	[ap]
coast	**ծովափ**	[ʦo'vap]
flow (flood tide)	**մակընթացություն**	[makıntaʦu'ʦyn]
ebb (ebb tide)	**տեղատվություն**	[tehatvu'ʦyn]
shoal	**առափնյա ծանծաղուտ**	[arap'ɲa ʦanʦa'hut]
bottom (~ of the sea)	**հատակ**	[a'tak]
wave	**ալիք**	[a'lik]
crest (~ of a wave)	**ալիքի կատար**	[ali'ki ka'tar]
spume (sea foam)	**փրփուր**	[prpur]
storm (sea storm)	**փոթորիկ**	[poto'rik]
hurricane	**մրրիկ**	[mrrik]
tsunami	**ցունամի**	[ʦu'nami]
calm (dead ~)	**խաղաղություն**	[hahahu'ʦyn]
quiet, calm (adj)	**հանգիստ**	[a'ŋist]
pole	**բևեռ**	[be'ver]
polar (adj)	**բևեռային**	[bevera'jın]
latitude	**լայնություն**	[lajnu'ʦyn]
longitude	**երկարություն**	[erkaru'ʦyn]
parallel	**զուգահեռական**	[zugaɛra'kan]
equator	**հասարակած**	[asara'kaʦ]
sky	**երկինք**	[er'kiŋk]
horizon	**հորիզոն**	[ori'zon]
air	**օդ**	[od]
lighthouse	**փարոս**	[pa'ros]
to dive (vi)	**սուզվել**	[suz'vel]
to sink (ab. boat)	**խորտակվել**	[hortak'vel]
treasures	**գանձեր**	[gan'ʤer]

78. Seas' and Oceans' names

Atlantic Ocean	**Ատլանտյան օվկիանոս**	[atlan'tʲan ovkia'nos]
Indian Ocean	**Հնդկական օվկիանոս**	[ɛndka'kan ovkia'nos]
Pacific Ocean	**Խաղաղ օվկիանոս**	[ha'hah ovkia'nos]
Arctic Ocean	**Հյուսիսային Սառուցյալ օվկիանոս**	[jusisa'jın saru'ʦʲal ovkia'nos]

Black Sea	Սև ծով	['sev 'tsov]
Red Sea	Կարմիր ծով	[kar'mir 'tsov]
Yellow Sea	Դեղին ծով	[de'hin 'tsov]
White Sea	Սպիտակ ծով	[spi'tak 'tsov]
Caspian Sea	Կասպից ծով	[kas'pits 'tsov]
Dead Sea	Մեռյալ ծով	[me'rʲal 'tsov]
Mediterranean Sea	Միջերկրական ծով	[midʒerkra'kan 'tsov]
Aegean Sea	Էգեյան ծով	[ɛge'jan 'tsov]
Adriatic Sea	Ադրիատիկ ծով	[adria'tik 'tsov]
Arabian Sea	Արաբական ծով	[araba'kan 'tsov]
Sea of Japan	Ճապոնական ծով	[tʃapona'kan 'tsov]
Bering Sea	Բերինգի ծով	[beri'ŋi 'tsov]
South China Sea	Արևելա-Չինական ծով	[areve'la tʃina'kan 'tsov]
Coral Sea	Կորալյան ծով	[kora'ʎan 'tsov]
Tasman Sea	Տասմանյան ծով	[tasma'ɲan 'tsov]
Caribbean Sea	Կարիբյան ծով	[kari'bʲan 'tsov]
Barents Sea	Բարենցյան ծով	[baren'tsʲan 'tsov]
Kara Sea	Կարսի ծով	[kar'si 'tsov]
North Sea	Հյուսիսային ծով	[jusisa'jɪn 'tsov]
Baltic Sea	Բալթիկ ծով	[bal'tik 'tsov]
Norwegian Sea	Նորվեգյան ծով	[norve'gʲan 'tsov]

79. Mountains

mountain	լեռ	[ler]
mountain range	լեռնաշղթա	[lernaʃh'ta]
mountain ridge	լեռնագագաթ	[lernaga'gat]
summit, top	գագաթ	[ga'gat]
peak	լեռնագագաթ	[lernaga'gat]
foot (~ of the mountain)	ստորոտ	[sto'rot]
slope (mountainside)	սարալանջ	[sara'landʒ]
volcano	հրաբուխ	[ɛra'buh]
active volcano	գործող հրաբուխ	[gor'tsoh ɛra'buh]
dormant volcano	հանգած հրաբուխ	[a'ŋats ɛra'buh]
eruption	ժայթքում	[ʒajt'kum]
crater	խառնարան	[harna'ran]
magma	մագմա	['magma]
lava	լավա	['lava]
molten (~ lava)	շիկացած	[ʃika'tsats]
canyon	խնձահովիտ	[hndzao'vit]
gorge	կիրճ	[kirtʃ]

crevice	նեղ կիրճ	[neh 'kirtʃ]
pass, col	լեռնանցք	[ler'nantsk]
plateau	սարահարթ	[sara'art]
cliff	ժայռ	[ʒajr]
hill	բլուր	[blur]
glacier	սառցադաշտ	[sartsa'daʃt]
waterfall	ջրվեժ	[dʒrveʒ]
geyser	գեյզեր	['gejzer]
lake	լիճ	[litʃ]
plain	հարթավայր	[arta'vajr]
landscape	բնատեսարան	[bnatesa'ran]
echo	արձագանք	[ardza'gaŋk]
alpinist	լեռնագնաց	[lernag'nats]
rock climber	ժայռամագլցող	[ʒajramagl'tsoh]
to conquer (in climbing)	գերել	[ge'rel]
climb (an easy ~)	վերելք	[ve'relk]

80. Mountains names

The Alps	Ալպեր	[aʎ'per]
Mont Blanc	Մոնբլան	[monb'lan]
The Pyrenees	Պիրինեյներ	[pirinej'ner]
The Carpathians	Կարպատներ	[karpat'ner]
The Ural Mountains	Ուրալյան լեռներ	[ura'ʎan ler'ner]
The Caucasus Mountains	Կովկաս	[kov'kas]
Mount Elbrus	Էլբրուս	[ɛʎb'rus]
The Altai Mountains	Այտայ	[al'taj]
The Tian Shan	Տյան Շան	[tʲan 'ʃʌn]
The Pamir Mountains	Պամիր	[pa'mir]
The Himalayas	Հիմալայներ	[imalaj'ner]
Mount Everest	Էվերեստ	[ɛve'rest]
The Andes	Անդեր	[an'der]
Mount Kilimanjaro	Կիլիմանջարո	[kiliman'dʒaro]

81. Rivers

river	գետ	[get]
spring (natural source)	աղբյուր	[ah'byr]
riverbed (river channel)	հուն	[un]
basin	ջրավազան	[dʒrava'zan]
to flow into ...	թափվել	[tap'vel]
tributary	վտակ	[vtak]

bank (of river)	ափ	[ap]
current (stream)	հոսանք	[o'saŋk]
downstream (adv)	հոսանքն ի վայր	[o'saŋkn 'i 'vajr]
upstream (adv)	հոսանքն ի վեր	[o'saŋkn 'i 'ver]
inundation	հեղեղում	[ɛhe'hum]
flooding	վարարություն	[vararu'ʦyn]
to overflow (vi)	վարարել	[vara'rel]
to flood (vt)	հեղեղել	[ɛhe'hel]
shallow (shoal)	ծանծաղուտ	[ʦanʦa'hut]
rapids	սահանք	[sa'aŋk]
dam	ամբարտակ	[ambar'tak]
canal	ջրանցք	[ʤ'ranʦk]
reservoir (artificial lake)	ջրամբար	[ʤram'bar]
sluice, lock	ջրագելակ	[ʤrage'lak]
water body (pond, etc.)	ջրավազան	[ʤrava'zan]
swamp (marshland)	ճահիճ	[ʧa'iʧ]
bog, marsh	ճահճուտ	[ʧah'ʧut]
whirlpool	հորձանուտ	[orʣa'nut]
stream (brook)	առու	[a'ru]
drinking (ab. water)	խմելու	[hme'lu]
fresh (~ water)	քաղցրահամ	[kahʦra'am]
ice	սառույց	[sa'rujʦ]
to freeze over (ab. river, etc.)	սառչել	[sar'ʧel]

82. Rivers' names

Seine	Սենա	['sena]
Loire	Լուարա	[lu'ara]
Thames	Թեմզա	['temza]
Rhine	Ռեյն	[rejn]
Danube	Դունայ	[du'naj]
Volga	Վոլգա	['volga]
Don	Դոն	[don]
Lena	Լենա	['lena]
Yellow River	Խուանխե	[huan'hɛ]
Yangtze	Յանցզի	[janʦ'zɪ]
Mekong	Մեկոնգ	[me'koŋ]
Ganges	Գանգես	[ga'ŋes]
Nile River	Նեղոս	[ne'hos]
Congo River	Կոնգո	['koŋo]

Okavango River	Օկավանգո	[oka'vaŋo]
Zambezi River	Զամբեզի	[zam'bezi]
Limpopo River	Լիմպոպո	[limpo'po]
Mississippi River	Միսիսիպի	[misisi'pi]

83. Forest

forest, wood	անտառ	[an'tar]
forest (as adj)	անտառային	[antara'jın]
thick forest	թավուտ	[ta'vut]
grove	պուրակ	[pu'rak]
forest clearing	բացատ	[ba'ʦat]
thicket	մացառուտ	[maʦa'rut]
scrubland	թփուտ	[tput]
footpath (troddenpath)	կածան	[ka'ʦan]
gully	ձորակ	[ʣo'rak]
tree	ծառ	[ʦar]
leaf	տերև	[te'rev]
leaves (foliage)	տերևներ	[terev'ner]
fall of leaves	տերևաթափ	[tereva'tap]
to fall (ab. leaves)	թափվել	[tap'vel]
top (of the tree)	կատար	[ka'tar]
branch	ճյուղ	[ʧuh]
bough	ոստ	[vost]
bud (on shrub, tree)	բողբոջ	[boh'boʤ]
needle (of pine tree)	փուշ	[puʃ]
pine cone	ելունդ	[e'lund]
hollow (in a tree)	փչակ	[pʧak]
nest	բույն	[bujn]
burrow (animal hole)	որջ	[vorʤ]
trunk	բուն	[bun]
root	արմատ	[ar'mat]
bark	կեղև	[ke'hev]
moss	մամուռ	[ma'mur]
to uproot (remove trees or tree stumps)	արմատախիլ անել	[armata'hil a'nel]
to chop down	հատել	[a'tel]
to deforest (vt)	անտառահատել	[antara:'tel]
tree stump	կոճղ	[koʧh]
campfire	խարույկ	[ha'rujk]
forest fire	հրդեհ	[ɛr'dɛ]

to extinguish (vt)	հանգցնել	[aŋʦ'nel]
forest ranger	անտառապահ	[antara'pa]
protection	պահպանություն	[pahpanu'ʦyn]
to protect (~ nature)	պահպանել	[pahpa'nel]
poacher	որսագող	[vorsa'goh]
steel trap	թակարդ	[ta'kard]
to gather, to pick (vt)	հավաքել	[ava'kel]
to lose one's way	մոլորվել	[molor'vel]

84. Natural resources

natural resources	բնական ռեսուրսներ	[bna'kan resurs'ner]
minerals	օգտակար հանածոներ	[ogta'kar anaʦo'ner]
deposits	հանքաշերտ	[aŋka'ʃərt]
field (e.g., oilfield)	հանքավայր	[aŋka'vajr]
to mine (extract)	արդյունահանել	[ardyna:'nel]
mining (extraction)	արդյունահանում	[ardyna:'num]
ore	հանքաքար	[aŋka'kar]
mine (e.g., for coal)	հանք	[aŋk]
shaft (mine ~)	հորան	[o'ran]
miner	հանքափոր	[aŋka'por]
gas (natural ~)	գազ	[gaz]
gas pipeline	գազատար	[gaza'tar]
oil (petroleum)	նավթ	[navt]
oil pipeline	նավթատար	[navta'tar]
oil well	նավթային աշտարակ	[navta'jın aʃta'rak]
derrick (tower)	հորատման աշտարակ	[orat'man aʃta'rak]
tanker	լցանավ	[lʦa'nav]
sand	ավազ	[a'vaz]
limestone	կրաքար	[kra'kar]
gravel	խիճ	[hiʧ]
peat	տորֆ	[torf]
clay	կավ	[kav]
coal	ածուխ	[a'ʦuh]
iron (ore)	երկաթ	[er'kat]
gold	ոսկի	[vos'ki]
silver	արծաթ	[ar'ʦat]
nickel	նիկել	[ni'kel]
copper	պղինձ	[phinʣ]
zinc	ցինկ	[ʦiŋk]
manganese	մանգան	[ma'ŋan]
mercury	սնդիկ	[sndik]
lead	արճիճ	[ar'ʧiʧ]

mineral	հանքանյութ	[aŋka'nyt]
crystal	բյուրեղ	[by'reh]
marble	մարմար	[mar'mar]
uranium	ուրան	[u'ran]

85. Weather

weather	եղանակ	[eha'nak]
weather forecast	եղանակի տեսություն	[ehana'ki tesu'tsyn]
temperature	ջերմաստիճան	[dʒermasti'tʃan]
thermometer	ջերմաչափ	[dʒerma'tʃap]
barometer	ծանրաչափ	[tsanra'tʃap]
humidity	խոնավություն	[honavu'tsyn]
heat (extreme ~)	տապ	[tap]
hot (torrid)	շոգ	[ʃog]
it's hot	շոգ է	['ʃog ɛ]
it's warm	տաք է	['tak ɛ]
warm (moderately hot)	տաք	[tak]
it's cold	ցուրտ է	['tsurt ɛ]
cold (adj)	սառը	['sarı]
sun	արև	[a'rev]
to shine (vi)	շողալ	[ʃo'hal]
sunny (day)	արևային	[areva'jın]
to come up (vi)	ծագել	[tsa'gel]
to set (vi)	մայր մտնել	['majr mt'nel]
cloud	ամպ	[amp]
cloudy (adj)	ամպամած	[ampa'mats]
rain cloud	թուխպ	[tuhp]
somber (gloomy)	ամպամած	[ampa'mats]
rain	անձրև	[andz'rev]
it's raining	անձրև է գալիս	[andz'rev ɛ ga'lis]
rainy (~ day, weather)	անձրևային	[andzreva'jın]
to drizzle (vi)	մաղել	[ma'hel]
pouring rain	տեղատարափ անձրև	[tehata'rap andz'rev]
downpour	տեղատարափ անձրև	[tehata'rap andz'rev]
heavy (e.g., ~ rain)	տարափ	[ta'rap]
puddle	ջրակույտ	[dʒra'kujt]
to get wet (in rain)	թրջվել	[trdʒvel]
fog (mist)	մառախուղ	[mara'huh]
foggy	մառախլապատ	[marahla'pat]
snow	ձյուն	[dzyn]
it's snowing	ձյուն է գալիս	['dzyn ɛ ga'lis]

86. Severe weather. Natural disasters

thunderstorm	փոթորիկ	[poto'rik]
lightning (~ strike)	կայծակ	[kaj'ʦak]
to flash (vi)	փայլատակել	[pajlata'kel]
thunder	որոտ	[vo'rot]
to thunder (vi)	որոտալ	[voro'tal]
it's thundering	ամպերը որոտում են	[am'perı voro'tum 'ɛn]
hail	կարկուտ	[kar'kut]
it's hailing	կարկուտ է գալիս	[kar'kut ɛ ga'lis]
to flood (vt)	հեղեղել	[ɛhe'hel]
flood, inundation	հեղեղում	[ɛhe'hum]
earthquake	երկրաշարժ	[erkra'ʃʌrʒ]
tremor, quake	ցնցում	[ʦnʦum]
epicenter	էպիկենտրոն	[ɛpikent'ron]
eruption	ժայթքում	[ʒajt'kum]
lava	լավա	['lava]
twister	մրրկասյուն	[mrrka'syn]
tornado	տորնադո	[tor'nado]
typhoon	տայֆուն	[taj'fun]
hurricane	մրրիկ	[mrrik]
storm	փոթորիկ	[poto'rik]
tsunami	ցունամի	[ʦu'nami]
cyclone	ցիկլոն	[ʦik'lon]
bad weather	վատ եղանակ	['vat eha'nak]
fire (accident)	հրդեհ	[ɛr'dɛ]
disaster	աղետ	[a'het]
meteorite	երկնաքար	[erkna'kar]
avalanche	հուսին	[u'sin]
snowslide	ձնահյուս	[ʣna'hys]
blizzard	բուք	[buk]
snowstorm	բորան	[bo'ran]

FAUNA

T&P Books Publishing

87. Mammals. Predators

predator	գիշատիչ	[giʃʌ'titʃ]
tiger	վագր	[vagr]
lion	առյուծ	[a'ryts]
wolf	գայլ	[gajl]
fox	աղվես	[ah'ves]
jaguar	հովազ	[o'vaz]
leopard	ընձառյուծ	[ɪndza'ryts]
cheetah	շնակատու	[ʃnaka'tu]
black panther	հովազ	[o'vaz]
puma	կուգուար	[kugu'ar]
snow leopard	ձյունաճերմակ հովազ	[dzynatʃer'mak o'vaz]
lynx	լուսան	[lu'san]
coyote	կոյոտ	[ko'jot]
jackal	շնագայլ	[ʃna'gajl]
hyena	բորենի	[bore'ni]

88. Wild animals

animal	կենդանի	[kenda'ni]
beast (animal)	գազան	[ga'zan]
squirrel	սկյուռ	[skyr]
hedgehog	ոզնի	[voz'ni]
hare	նապաստակ	[napas'tak]
rabbit	ճագար	[tʃa'gar]
badger	փորսուղ	[por'suh]
raccoon	ջրարջ	[dʒrardʒ]
hamster	գերմանամուկ	[germana'muk]
marmot	արջամուկ	[ardʒa'muk]
mole	խլուրդ	[hlurd]
mouse	մուկ	[muk]
rat	առնետ	[ar'net]
bat	չղջիկ	[tʃhdʒik]
ermine	կնգում	[kŋum]
sable	սամույր	[sa'mujr]
marten	կզաքիս	[kza'kis]

weasel	աքիս	[a'kis]
mink	ջրաքիս	[ʤra'kis]
beaver	կուղբ	[kuhb]
otter	ջրասամույր	[ʤrasa'mujr]
horse	ձի	[ʣi]
moose	որմզդեղն	[vormz'dehn]
deer	եղջերու	[ehʤe'ru]
camel	ուղտ	[uht]
bison	բիզոն	[bi'zon]
aurochs	վայրի ցուլ	[vaj'ri 'ʦul]
buffalo	գոմեշ	[go'meʃ]
zebra	զեբր	[zebr]
antelope	այծեղջերու	[ajʦehʤe'ru]
roe deer	այծյամ	[aj'ʦʲam]
fallow deer	եղնիկ	[eh'nik]
chamois	քարայծ	[ka'rajʦ]
wild boar	վարազ	[va'raz]
whale	կետ	[ket]
seal	փոկ	[pok]
walrus	ծովափիղ	[ʦova'pih]
fur seal	ծովարջ	[ʦo'varʤ]
dolphin	դելֆին	[deʎ'fin]
bear	արջ	[arʤ]
polar bear	սպիտակ արջ	[spi'tak 'arʤ]
panda	պանդա	['panda]
monkey	կապիկ	[ka'pik]
chimpanzee	շիմպանզե	[ʃimpan'ze]
orangutan	օրանգուտանգ	[oraŋu'taŋ]
gorilla	գորիլլա	[go'rilla]
macaque	մակակա	[ma'kaka]
gibbon	գիբբոն	[gib'bon]
elephant	փիղ	[pih]
rhinoceros	ռնգեղջյուր	[rŋeh'ʤyr]
giraffe	ընձուղտ	[ɪn'ʣuht]
hippopotamus	գետաձի	[geta'ʣi]
kangaroo	ագևազ	[age'vaz]
koala (bear)	կոալա	[ko'ala]
mongoose	մանգուստ	[ma'ŋust]
chinchilla	շինշիլա	[ʃin'ʃila]
skunk	սկունս	[skuns]
porcupine	խոզուկ	[ho'zuk]

89. Domestic animals

cat	կատու	[ka'tu]
tomcat	կատու	[ka'tu]
dog	շուն	[ʃun]
horse	ձի	[ʣi]
stallion	հովատակ	[ova'tak]
mare	զամբիկ	[zam'bik]
cow	կով	[kov]
bull	ցուլ	[ʦul]
ox	եզ	[ez]
sheep (ewe)	ոչխար	[voʧ'har]
ram	խոյ	[hoj]
goat	այծ	[ajʦ]
billy goat, he-goat	այծ	[ajʦ]
donkey	ավանակ	[ava'nak]
mule	ջորի	[ʤo'ri]
pig, hog	խոզ	[hoz]
piglet	գոճի	[go'ʧi]
rabbit	ճագար	[ʧa'gar]
hen (chicken)	հավ	[av]
rooster	աքլոր	[ak'lor]
duck	բադ	[bad]
drake	բադաքլոր	[badak'lor]
goose	սագ	[sag]
tom turkey, gobbler	հնդկահավ	[ɪndka'av]
turkey (hen)	հնդկահավ	[ɪndka'av]
domestic animals	ընտանի կենդանիներ	[ɪnta'ni kendani'ner]
tame (e.g., ~ hamster)	ձեռնասուն	[ʣerna'sun]
to tame (vt)	ընտելացնել	[ɪntelaʦ'nel]
to breed (vt)	բուծել	[bu'ʦel]
farm	ֆերմա	['ferma]
poultry	ընտանի թռչուններ	[ɪnta'ni trʧu'ŋer]
cattle	անասուն	[ana'sun]
herd (cattle)	նախիր	[na'hir]
stable	ախոռ	[a'hor]
pigsty	խոզանոց	[hoza'noʦ]
cowshed	գոմ	[gom]
rabbit hutch	ճագարանոց	[ʧagara'noʦ]
hen house	հավանոց	[ava'noʦ]

90. Birds

bird	թռչուն	[trʧun]
pigeon	աղավնի	[ahav'ni]
sparrow	ճնճղուկ	[ʧnʧhuk]
tit	երաշտահավ	[eraʃta'av]
magpie	կաչաղակ	[kaʧa'hak]
raven	ագռավ	[ag'rav]
crow	ագռավ	[ag'rav]
jackdaw	ճայակ	[ʧa'jak]
rook	սերմնագռավ	[sermnag'rav]
duck	բադ	[bad]
goose	սագ	[sag]
pheasant	փասիան	[pasi'an]
eagle	արծիվ	[ar'ʦiv]
hawk	շահեն	[ʃʌ'ɛn]
falcon	բազե	[ba'ze]
vulture	անգղ	[aŋh]
condor (Andean ~)	պասկուճ	[pas'kuʧ]
swan	կարապ	[ka'rap]
crane	կռունկ	[kruŋk]
stork	արագիլ	[ara'gil]
parrot	թութակ	[tu'tak]
hummingbird	կոլիբրի	[ko'libri]
peacock	սիրամարգ	[sira'marg]
ostrich	ջայլամ	[ʤaj'lam]
heron	ձկնկուլ	[dzkŋkul]
flamingo	վարդաթևիկ	[vardate'vik]
pelican	հավալուսն	[ava'lusn]
nightingale	սոխակ	[so'hak]
swallow	ծիծեռնակ	[ʦiʦer'nak]
thrush	կեռնեխ	[ker'neh]
song thrush	երգող կեռնեխ	[er'goh ker'neh]
blackbird	սև կեռնեխ	['sev ker'neh]
swift	ջրածիծառ	[ʤraʦi'ʦar]
lark	արտույտ	[ar'tujt]
quail	լոր	[lor]
woodpecker	փայտփորիկ	[pajtpo'rik]
cuckoo	կկու	[kɪ'ku]
owl	բու	[bu]
eagle owl	բվեճ	[bveʧ]

wood grouse	խլահավ	[hla'av]
black grouse	ցախաքլոր	[tsahak'lor]
partridge	կաքավ	[ka'kav]
starling	սարյակ	[sa'rʲak]
canary	դեղձանիկ	[dehdza'nik]
hazel grouse	աքար	[a'kar]
chaffinch	սերինոս	[seri'nos]
bullfinch	խածկտիկ	[hatsk'tik]
seagull	ճայ	[tʃaj]
albatross	ալբատրոս	[aʎbat'ros]
penguin	պինգվին	[piŋ'vin]

91. Fish. Marine animals

bream	բրամ	[bram]
carp	գետածածան	[getatsa'tsan]
perch	պերկես	[per'kes]
catfish	լոքո	[lo'ko]
pike	գայլաձուկ	[gajla'dzuk]
salmon	սաղման	[sah'man]
sturgeon	թառափ	[ta'rap]
herring	ծովատառեխ	[tsovata'reh]
Atlantic salmon	սաղման ձուկ	[sah'man 'dzuk]
mackerel	թյունիկ	[ty'nik]
flatfish	տափակաձուկ	[tapaka'dzuk]
zander, pike perch	շիղաձուկ	[ʃiha'dzuk]
cod	ձողաձուկ	[dzoha'dzuk]
tuna	թյունոս	[ty'ŋos]
trout	իշխան	[iʃ'han]
eel	օձաձուկ	[odza'dzuk]
electric ray	էլեկտրավոր կատվաձուկ	[ɛlektra'vor katva'dzuk]
moray eel	մուրենա	[mu'rena]
piranha	պիրանյա	[pi'raɲja]
shark	շնաձուկ	[ʃna'dzuk]
dolphin	դելֆին	[deʎ'fin]
whale	կետ	[ket]
crab	ծովախեցգետին	[tsovahetsge'tin]
jellyfish	մեդուզա	[me'duza]
octopus	ութոտնուկ	[utvot'nuk]
starfish	ծովաստղ	[tso'vasth]
sea urchin	ծովոզնի	[tsovoz'ni]

seahorse	ծովաձի	[tsova'dzi]
oyster	ոստրե	[vost're]
shrimp	մանր ծովախեցգետին	['manr tsovahetsge'tin]
lobster	օմար	[o'mar]
spiny lobster	լանգուստ	[la'ŋust]

92. Amphibians. Reptiles

snake	օձ	[odz]
venomous (snake)	թունավոր	[tuna'vor]
viper	իժ	[iʒ]
cobra	կոբրա	['kobra]
python	պիթոն	[pi'ton]
boa	վիշապօձ	[viʃʌ'podz]
grass snake	լորտու	[lor'tu]
rattle snake	խարամանի	[harama'ni]
anaconda	անակոնդա	[ana'konda]
lizard	մողես	[mo'hes]
iguana	իգուանա	[igu'ana]
monitor lizard	վարան	[va'ran]
salamander	սալամանդր	[sala'mandr]
chameleon	քամելեոն	[kamele'on]
scorpion	կարիճ	[ka'ritʃ]
turtle	կրիա	[kri'a]
frog	գորտ	[gort]
toad	դոդոշ	[do'doʃ]
crocodile	կոկորդիլոս	[kokordi'los]

93. Insects

insect, bug	միջատ	[mi'dʒat]
butterfly	թիթեռ	[ti'ter]
ant	մրջյուն	[mrdʒun]
fly	ճանճ	[tʃantʃ]
mosquito	մոծակ	[mo'tsak]
beetle	բզեզ	[bzez]
wasp	իշամեղու	[iʃʌme'hu]
bee	մեղու	[me'hu]
bumblebee	կրետ	[kret]
gadfly	բոռ	[bor]
spider	սարդ	[sard]
spider's web	սարդոստայն	[sardos'tajn]

dragonfly	ճպուռ	[ʧpur]
grasshopper	մորեխ	[mo'reh]
moth (night butterfly)	թիթեռնիկ	[titer'nik]
cockroach	ուտիճ	[u'tiʧ]
tick	տիզ	[tiz]
flea	լու	[lu]
midge	մլակ	[mlak]
locust	մարախ	[ma'rah]
snail	խխունջ	[hı'hunʤ]
cricket	ծղրիդ	[ʦshrid]
lightning bug	լուսատիտիկ	[lusati'tik]
ladybug	զատիկ	[za'tik]
cockchafer	մայիսյան բզեզ	[majı'sʲan b'zez]
leech	տզրուկ	[tzruk]
caterpillar	թրթուր	[trtur]
earthworm	որդ	[vord]
larva	թրթուր	[trtur]

FLORA

T&P Books Publishing

94. Trees

tree	ծառ	[ʦar]
deciduous (adj)	սաղարթավոր	[saharta'vor]
coniferous (adj)	փշատերև	[pʃʌte'rev]
evergreen (adj)	մշտադալար	[mʃtada'lar]
apple tree	խնձորենի	[hnʣore'ni]
pear tree	տանձենի	[tanʣe'ni]
sweet cherry tree	կեռասենի	[kerase'ni]
sour cherry tree	բալենի	[bale'ni]
plum tree	սալորենի	[salore'ni]
birch	կեչի	[ke'ʧi]
oak	կաղնի	[kah'ni]
linden tree	լորի	[lo'ri]
aspen	կաղամախի	[kahama'hi]
maple	թխկի	[thki]
spruce	եղևնի	[ehev'ni]
pine	սոճի	[so'ʧi]
larch	կուենի	[kue'ni]
fir tree	բրգաձև սոճի	[brga'ʣev so'ʧi]
cedar	մայրի	[maj'ri]
poplar	բարդի	[bar'di]
rowan	սնձենի	[snʣe'ni]
willow	ուռենի	[ure'ni]
alder	լաստենի	[laste'ni]
beech	հաճարենի	[aʧare'ni]
elm	ծփի	[ʦpi]
ash (tree)	հացենի	[aʦe'ni]
chestnut	շագանակենի	[ʃʌganake'ni]
magnolia	կղբի	[khbi]
palm tree	արմավենի	[armave'ni]
cypress	նոճի	[no'ʧi]
mangrove	մանգրածառ	[maŋra'ʦar]
baobab	բաոբաբ	[bao'bab]
eucalyptus	էվկալիպտ	[ɛvka'lipt]
sequoia	սեկվոյա	[sek'voja]

95. Shrubs

bush	թուփ	[tup]
shrub	թփուտ	[tput]
grapevine	խաղող	[ha'hoh]
vineyard	խաղողի այգի	[haho'hi aj'gi]
raspberry bush	մորի	[mo'ri]
redcurrant bush	կարմիր հաղարջ	[kar'mir a'hardʒ]
gooseberry bush	հաղարջ	[a'hardʒ]
acacia	ակացիա	[a'katsia]
barberry	ծորենի	[tsore'ni]
jasmine	հասմիկ	[as'mik]
juniper	գիհի	[gi'hi]
rosebush	վարդենի	[varde'ni]
dog rose	մասուր	[ma'sur]

96. Fruits. Berries

apple	խնձոր	[hndzor]
pear	տանձ	[tandz]
plum	սալոր	[sa'lor]
strawberry	ելակ	[e'lak]
sour cherry	բալ	[bal]
sweet cherry	կեռաս	[ke'ras]
grape	խաղող	[ha'hoh]
raspberry	մորի	[mo'ri]
blackcurrant	սև հաղարջ	['sev a'hardʒ]
redcurrant	կարմիր հաղարջ	[kar'mir a'hardʒ]
gooseberry	հաղարջ	[a'hardʒ]
cranberry	լոռամրգի	[loramr'gi]
orange	նարինջ	[na'rindʒ]
mandarin	մանդարին	[manda'rin]
pineapple	արքայախնձոր	[arkajahn'dzor]
banana	բանան	[ba'nan]
date	արմավ	[ar'mav]
lemon	կիտրոն	[kit'ron]
apricot	ծիրան	[tsi'ran]
peach	դեղձ	[dehdz]
kiwi	կիվի	['kivi]
grapefruit	գրեյպֆրուտ	[grejpf'rut]
berry	հատապտուղ	[atap'tuh]

berries	հատապտուղներ	[ataptuh'ner]
cowberry	հապալաս	[apa'las]
field strawberry	վայրի ելակ	[vaj'ri e'lak]
bilberry	հապալաս	[apa'las]

97. Flowers. Plants

flower	ծաղիկ	[tsa'hik]
bouquet (of flowers)	ծաղկեփունջ	[tsahke'pundʒ]
rose (flower)	վարդ	[vard]
tulip	վարդակակաչ	[vardaka'katʃ]
carnation	մեխակ	[me'hak]
gladiolus	թրաշուշան	[traʃu'ʃʌn]
cornflower	կապույտ տերեփուկ	[ka'pujt tere'puk]
bluebell	զանգակ	[za'ŋak]
dandelion	կաթնուկ	[kat'nuk]
camomile	երիցուկ	[eri'tsuk]
aloe	ալոե	[a'loɛ]
cactus	կակտուս	['kaktus]
rubber plant, ficus	ֆիկուս	['fikus]
lily	շուշան	[ʃu'ʃʌn]
geranium	խորդենի	[horde'ni]
hyacinth	հակինթ	[a'kint]
mimosa	պատկառուկ	[patka'ruk]
narcissus	նարգիզ	[nar'giz]
nasturtium	ջրկոտեմ	[dʒrko'tem]
orchid	խոլորձ	[ho'lordz]
peony	քաջվարդ	[kadʒ'vard]
violet	մանուշակ	[manu'ʃʌk]
pansy	եռագույն մանուշակ	[era'gujn manu'ʃʌk]
forget-me-not	անմոռուկ	[anmo'ruk]
daisy	մարգարտածաղիկ	[margartatsa'hik]
poppy	կակաչ	[ka'katʃ]
hemp	կանեփ	[ka'nep]
mint	անանուխ	[ana'nuh]
lily of the valley	հովտաշուշան	[ovtaʃu'ʃʌn]
snowdrop	ձնծաղիկ	[dzntsa'hik]
nettle	եղինջ	[e'hindʒ]
sorrel	թրթնջուկ	[trtndʒuk]
water lily	ջրաշուշան	[dʒraʃu'ʃʌn]

fern	ձարխոտ	[dzar'hot]
lichen	քարաքոս	[kara'kos]
greenhouse (tropical ~)	ջերմոց	[dʒer'mots]
lawn	գազոն	[ga'zon]
flowerbed	ծաղկաթումբ	[tsahka'tumb]
plant	բույս	[bujs]
grass	խոտ	[hot]
blade of grass	խոտիկ	[ho'tik]
leaf	տերև	[te'rev]
petal	թերթիկ	[ter'tik]
stem	ցողուն	[tso'hun]
tuber	պալար	[pa'lar]
young plant (shoot)	ծիլ	[tsil]
thorn	փուշ	[puʃ]
to blossom (vi)	ծաղկել	[tsah'kel]
to fade, to wither	թոշնել	[trʃnel]
smell (odor)	բուրմունք	[bur'muŋk]
to cut (flowers)	կտրել	[ktrel]
to pick (a flower)	պոկել	[po'kel]

98. Cereals, grains

grain	հացահատիկ	[atsa:'tik]
cereal crops	հացահատիկային բույսեր	[atsa:tika'jın buj'ser]
ear (of barley, etc.)	հասկ	[ask]
wheat	ցորեն	[tso'ren]
rye	տարեկան	[tare'kan]
oats	վարսակ	[var'sak]
millet	կորեկ	[ko'rek]
barley	գարի	[ga'ri]
corn	եգիպտացորեն	[egiptatso'ren]
rice	բրինձ	[brindz]
buckwheat	հնդկացորեն	[ındkatso'ren]
pea plant	սիսեռ	[si'ser]
kidney bean	լոբի	[lo'bi]
soy	սոյա	[so'ja]
lentil	ոսպ	[vosp]
beans (pulse crops)	լոբազգիներ	[lobazgi'ner]

COUNTRIES OF THE WORLD

T&P Books Publishing

99. Countries. Part 1

Afghanistan	Աֆղանստան	[afhans'tan]
Albania	Ալբանիա	[al'bania]
Argentina	Արգենտինա	[argen'tina]
Armenia	Հայաստան	[ajas'tan]
Australia	Ավստրալիա	[avst'ralia]
Austria	Ավստրիա	[avstria]
Azerbaijan	Ադրբեջան	[adrbe'ʤan]
The Bahamas	Բահամյան կղզիներ	[ba:'mʲan khzi'ner]
Bangladesh	Բանգլադեշ	[baŋla'deʃ]
Belarus	Բելառուս	[bela'rus]
Belgium	Բելգիա	['beʎgia]
Bolivia	Բոլիվիա	[bo'livia]
Bosnia and Herzegovina	Բոսնիա և Հերցեգովինա	['bosnia 'ev ɛrʦego'vina]
Brazil	Բրազիլիա	[bra'zilia]
Bulgaria	Բուլղարիա	[bul'haria]
Cambodia	Կամպուչիա	[kampu'ʧia]
Canada	Կանադա	[ka'nada]
Chile	Չիլի	['ʧili]
China	Չինաստան	[ʧinas'tan]
Colombia	Կոլումբիա	[ko'lumbia]
Croatia	Խորվաթիա	[hor'vatia]
Cuba	Կուբա	['kuba]
Cyprus	Կիպրոս	[kip'ros]
Czech Republic	Չեխիա	['ʧehia]
Denmark	Դանիա	['dania]
Dominican Republic	Դոմինիկյան հանրապետություն	[domini'kʲan anrapetu'ʦyn]
Ecuador	Էկվադոր	[ɛkva'dor]
Egypt	Եգիպտոս	[egip'tos]
England	Անգլիա	['aŋlia]
Estonia	Էստոնիա	[ɛs'tonia]
Finland	Ֆինլանդիա	[fin'landia]
France	Ֆրանսիա	[f'ransia]
French Polynesia	Ֆրանսիական Պոլինեզիա	[fransia'kan poli'nezia]
Georgia	Վրաստան	[vras'tan]
Germany	Գերմանիա	[ger'mania]
Ghana	Գանա	['gana]
Great Britain	Մեծ Բրիտանիա	['meʦ bri'tania]
Greece	Հունաստան	[unas'tan]
Haiti	Հաիթի	[ai'ti]
Hungary	Վենգրիա	['veŋria]

100. Countries. Part 2

Iceland	Իսլանդիա	[is'landia]
India	Հնդկաստան	[ındkas'tan]
Indonesia	Ինդոնեզի	[indo'nezia]
Iran	Պարսկաստան	[parskas'tan]
Iraq	Իրաք	[i'rak]
Ireland	Իռլանդիա	[ir'landia]
Israel	Իսրայել	[isra'jel]
Italy	Իտալիա	[i'talia]
Jamaica	Ցամայկա	[ja'majka]
Japan	Ճապոնիա	[ʧa'ponia]
Jordan	Հորդանան	[orda'nan]
Kazakhstan	Ղազախստան	[hazahs'tan]
Kenya	Քենիա	['kenia]
Kirghizia	Ղրղզստան	[hrhzstan]
Kuwait	Քուվեյթ	[ku'vejt]
Laos	Լաոս	[la'os]
Latvia	Լատվիա	['latvia]
Lebanon	Լիբանան	[liba'nan]
Libya	Լիբիա	['libia]
Liechtenstein	Լիխտենշտայն	[lihtenʃ'tajn]
Lithuania	Լիտվա	[lit'va]
Luxembourg	Լյուքսեմբուրգ	[lyksem'burg]
Macedonia (Republic of ~)	Մակեդոնիա	[make'donia]
Madagascar	Մադագասկար	[madagas'kar]
Malaysia	Մալայզիա	[ma'lajzia]
Malta	Մալթա	['maʎta]
Mexico	Մեքսիկա	['meksika]
Moldova, Moldavia	Մոլդովա	[mol'dova]
Monaco	Մոնակո	[mo'nako]
Mongolia	Մոնղոլիա	[mon'holia]
Montenegro	Չեռնոգորիա	[ʧerno'goria]
Morocco	Մարոկկո	[ma'rokko]
Myanmar	Մյանմար	[mjan'mar]
Namibia	Նամիբիա	[na'mibia]
Nepal	Նեպալ	[ne'pal]
Netherlands	Նիդեռլանդներ	[niderland'ner]
New Zealand	Նոր Զելանդիա	['nor ze'landia]
North Korea	Հյուսիսային Կորեա	[jusisa'jın ko'rea]
Norway	Նորվեգիա	[nor'vegia]

101. Countries. Part 3

Pakistan	Պակիստան	[pakis'tan]
Palestine	Պաղեստինյան ինքնավարություն	[pahesti'ɲan iŋknavaru'ʦyn]

Panama	Պանամա	[pa'nama]
Paraguay	Պարագվայ	[parag'vaj]
Peru	Պերու	[pe'ru]
Poland	Լեհաստան	[leas'tan]
Portugal	Պորտուգալիա	[portu'galia]
Romania	Ռումինիա	[ru'minia]
Russia	Ռուսաստան	[rusas'tan]
Saudi Arabia	Սաուդյան Արաբիա	[sau'dʲan a'rabia]
Scotland	Շոտլանդիա	[ʃot'landia]
Senegal	Սենեգալ	[sene'gal]
Serbia	Սերբիա	['serbia]
Slovakia	Սլովակիա	[slo'vakia]
Slovenia	Սլովենիա	[slo'venia]
South Africa	Հարավ-Աֆրիկյան հանրապետություն	[a'rav afri'kʲan anrapetu'ʦyn]
South Korea	Հարավային Կորեա	[arava'jɪn ko'rea]
Spain	Իսպանիա	[is'pania]
Suriname	Սուրինամ	[suri'nam]
Sweden	Շվեդիա	[ʃ'vedia]
Switzerland	Շվեյցարիա	[ʃvej'ʦaria]
Syria	Սիրիա	['siria]
Taiwan	Թայվան	[taj'van]
Tajikistan	Տաջիկստան	[taʤiks'tan]
Tanzania	Տանզանիա	[tan'zania]
Tasmania	Տասմանիա	[tas'mania]
Thailand	Թաիլանդ	[tai'land]
Tunisia	Թունիս	[tu'nis]
Turkey	Թուրքիա	['turkia]
Turkmenistan	Թուրքմենստան	[turkmens'tan]
Ukraine	Ուկրաինա	[ukra'ina]
United Arab Emirates	Միավորված Արաբական Էմիրություններ	[miavor'vaʦ araba'kan ɛmiruʦy'ŋer]
United States of America	Ամերիկայի Միացյալ Նահանգներ	[amerika'jɪ mia'ʦʲal na:'ŋer]
Uruguay	Ուրուգվայ	[urug'vaj]
Uzbekistan	Ուզբեկստան	[uzbeks'tan]
Vatican	Վատիկան	[vati'kan]
Venezuela	Վենեսուելա	[venesu'ɛla]
Vietnam	Վիետնամ	[vjet'nam]
Zanzibar	Զանզիբար	[zanzi'bar]

GASTRONOMIC GLOSSARY

This section contains a lot of words and terms associated with food. This dictionary will make it easier for you to understand the menu at a restaurant and choose the right dish

T&P Books Publishing

English-Armenian gastronomic glossary

aftertaste	կողմնակի համ	[kohmna'ki 'am]
almond	նուշ	[nuʃ]
anise	անիսոն	[ani'son]
aperitif	ապերիտիվ	[aperi'tiv]
appetite	ախորժակ	[ahor'ʒak]
appetizer	խորտիկ	[hor'tik]
apple	խնձոր	[hndzor]
apricot	ծիրան	[tsi'ran]
artichoke	արտիճուկ	[arti'tʃuk]
asparagus	ծնեբեկ	[tsne'bek]
Atlantic salmon	սաղման ձուկ	[sah'man 'dzuk]
avocado	ավոկադո	[avo'kado]
bacon	բեկոն	[be'kon]
banana	բանան	[ba'nan]
barley	գարի	[ga'ri]
bartender	բարմեն	[bar'men]
basil	ռեհան	[re'han]
bay leaf	դափնու տերև	[dap'nu te'rev]
beans	լոբի	[lo'bi]
beef	տավարի միս	[tava'ri 'mis]
beer	գարեջուր	[gare'dʒur]
beetroot	բազուկ	[ba'zuk]
bell pepper	պղպեղ	[phpeh]
berries	հատապտուղներ	[ataptuh'ner]
berry	հատապտուղ	[atap'tuh]
bilberry	հապալաս	[apa'las]
birch bolete	ժանտասունկ	[ʒanta'suŋk]
bitter	դառը	['darı]
black coffee	սև սուրճ	[sev 'surtʃ]
black pepper	սև պղպեղ	[sev ph'peh]
black tea	սև թեյ	[sev 'tej]
blackberry	մոշ	[moʃ]
blackcurrant	սև հաղարջ	['sev a'hardʒ]
boiled	եփած	[e'pats]
bottle opener	բացիչ	[ba'tsitʃ]
bread	հաց	[hats]
breakfast	նախաճաշ	[naha'tʃaʃ]
bream	բրամ	[bram]
broccoli	կաղամբ բրոկոլի	[ka'hamb bro'koli]
Brussels sprouts	բրյուսելյան կաղամբ	[bryse'ʎan ka'hamb]
buckwheat	հնդկացորեն	[ındkatso'ren]
butter	սերուցքային կարագ	[serutska'jın ka'rag]
buttercream	կրեմ	[krem]
cabbage	կաղամբ	[ka'hamb]

cake	հրուշակ	[ɛru'ʃʌk]
cake	տորթ	[tort]
calorie	կալորիա	[ka'lorija]
can opener	բացիչ	[ba'tsitʃ]
candy	կոնֆետ	[kon'fet]
canned food	պահածոներ	[pa:tso'ner]
cappuccino	սերուցքով սուրճ	[seruts'kov 'surtʃ]
caraway	չաման	[tʃa'man]
carbohydrates	ածխաջրեր	[atshadʒ'rer]
carbonated	գազավորված	[gazavor'vats]
carp	գետածածան	[getatsa'tsan]
carrot	գազար	[ga'zar]
catfish	լոքո	[lo'ko]
cauliflower	ծաղկակաղամբ	[tsahkaka'hamb]
caviar	ձկնկիթ	[dzkŋkit]
celery	նեխուր	[ne'hur]
cep	սպիտակ սունկ	[spi'tak 'suŋk]
cereal crops	հացահատիկային բույսեր	[atsa:tika'jɪn buj'ser]
cereal grains	ձավար	[dza'var]
champagne	շամպայն	[ʃʌm'pajn]
chanterelle	ձվասունկ	[dzva'suŋk]
check	հաշիվ	[a'ʃiv]
cheese	պանիր	[pa'nir]
chewing gum	մաստակ	[mas'tak]
chicken	հավ	[av]
chocolate	շոկոլադ	[ʃoko'lad]
chocolate	շոկոլադե	[ʃokola'dɛ]
cinnamon	դարչին	[dar'tʃin]
clear soup	մսաջուր	[msa'dʒur]
cloves	մեխակ	[me'hak]
cocktail	կոկտեյլ	[kok'tejʎ]
coconut	կոկոսի ընկույզ	[ko'kosi ɪ'ŋkujz]
cod	ձողաձուկ	[dzoha'dzuk]
coffee	սուրճ	[surtʃ]
coffee with milk	կաթով սուրճ	[ka'tov 'surtʃ]
cognac	կոնյակ	[ko'ɲjak]
cold	սառը	['sarɪ]
condensed milk	խտացրած կաթ	[htats'rats 'kat]
condiment	համեմունք	[ame'muŋk]
confectionery	հրուշակեղեն	[ɛruʃʌke'hen]
cookies	թխվածքաբլիթ	[thvatskab'lit]
coriander	գինձ	[gindz]
corkscrew	խցանահան	[htsana'an]
corn	եգիպտացորեն	[egiptatso'ren]
corn	եգիպտացորեն	[egiptatso'ren]
cornflakes	եգիպտացորենի փաթիլներ	[egiptatsore'ni patil'ner]
course, dish	ճաշատեսակ	[tʃaʃʌte'sak]
cowberry	հապալաս	[apa'las]
crab	ծովախեցգետին	[tsovahetsge'tin]
cranberry	լոռամրգի	[loramr'gi]
cream	սերուցք	[se'rutsk]

crumb	փշուր	[pʃur]
cucumber	վարունգ	[va'ruŋ]
cuisine	խոհանոց	[hoa'nots]
cup	բաժակ	[ba'ʒak]
dark beer	մուգ գարեջուր	['mug gare'dʒur]
date	արմավ	[ar'mav]
death cap	թունավոր սունկ	[tuna'vor 'suŋk]
dessert	աղանդեր	[ahan'der]
diet	սննդակարգ	[sŋda'karg]
dill	սամիթ	[sa'mit]
dinner	ընթրիք	[ɪnt'rik]
dried	չորացրած	[tʃorats'rats]
drinking water	խմելու ջուր	[hme'lu 'dʒur]
duck	բադ	[bad]
ear	հասկ	[ask]
edible mushroom	ուտելու սունկ	[ute'lu 'suŋk]
eel	օձաձուկ	[odza'dzuk]
egg	ձու	[dzu]
egg white	սպիտակուց	[spita'kuts]
egg yolk	դեղնուց	[deh'nuts]
eggplant	սմբուկ	[smbuk]
eggs	ձվեր	[dzver]
Enjoy your meal!	Բարի՜ ախորժակ:	[ba'ri ahor'ʒak]
fats	ճարպեր	[tʃar'per]
field strawberry	վայրի ելակ	[vaj'ri e'lak]
fig	թուզ	[tuz]
filling	լցոն	[ltson]
fish	ձուկ	[dzuk]
flatfish	տափակաձուկ	[tapaka'dzuk]
flour	ալյուր	[a'lyr]
fly agaric	ճանճասպան	[tʃantʃas'pan]
food	կերակուր	[kera'kur]
fork	պատառաքաղ	[patara'kah]
freshly squeezed juice	թարմ քամված հյութ	['tarm kam'vats h'jut]
fried	տապակած	[tapa'kats]
fried eggs	ձվածեղ	[dzva'tseh]
fried meatballs	կոտլետ	[kot'let]
frozen	սառեցված	[sarets'vats]
fruit	միրգ	[mirg]
game	որսամիս	[vorsa'mis]
gammon	ազդր	[azdr]
garlic	սխտոր	[shtor]
gin	ջին	[dʒin]
ginger	իմբիր	[im'birʲ]
glass	բաժակ	[ba'ʒak]
glass	գավաթ	[ga'vat]
goose	սագ	[sag]
gooseberry	հաղարջ	[a'hardʒ]
grain	հացահատիկ	[atsa:'tik]
grape	խաղող	[ha'hoh]
grapefruit	գրեյպֆրուտ	[grejpf'rut]
green tea	կանաչ թեյ	[ka'natʃ 'tej]

greens	կանաչի	[kana'tʃi]
halibut	վահանաձուկ	[va:na'dzuk]
ham	խոզապուխտ	[hoza'puht]
hamburger	աղացած միս	[aha'tsats 'mis]
hamburger	համբուրգեր	[ambur'ger]
hazelnut	պնդուկ	[pnduk]
herring	ծովատառեխ	[tsovata'reh]
honey	մեղր	[mehr]
horseradish	ծովաբողկ	[tsova'bohk]
hot	տաք	[tak]
ice	սառույց	[sa'rujts]
ice-cream	պաղպաղակ	[pahpa'hak]
instant coffee	լուծվող սուրճ	[luts'voh 'surtʃ]
jam	ջեմ	[dʒem]
jam	մուրաբա	[mura'ba]
juice	հյութ	[hjut]
kidney bean	լոբի	[lo'bi]
kiwi	կիվի	['kivi]
knife	դանակ	[da'nak]
lamb	ոչխարի միս	[votʃha'ri 'mis]
lard	սալ	[sal]
lemon	կիտրոն	[kit'ron]
lemonade	լիմոնադ	[limo'nad]
lentil	ոսպ	[vosp]
lettuce	սալաթ	[sa'lat]
light beer	բաց գարեջուր	['bats gare'dʒur]
liqueur	լիկյոր	[li'kɜr]
liquors	ալկոհոլային խմիչքներ	[alko:la'jın hmitʃk'ner]
liver	լյարդ	[ʎard]
lunch	ճաշ	[tʃaʃ]
mackerel	թյունիկ	[ty'nik]
mandarin	մանդարին	[manda'rin]
mango	մանգո	['maŋo]
margarine	մարգարին	[marga'rin]
marmalade	մարմելադ	[marme'lad]
mashed potatoes	կարտոֆիլի պյուրե	[kartofi'li py're]
mayonnaise	մայոնեզ	[majo'nez]
meat	միս	[mis]
melon	սեխ	[seh]
menu	մենյու	[me'ny]
milk	կաթ	[kat]
milkshake	կաթնային կոկտեյլ	[katna'jın kok'tejʎ]
millet	կորեկ	[ko'rek]
mineral water	հանքային ջուր	[aŋka'jın 'dʒur]
morel	մորխ	[morh]
mushroom	սունկ	[suŋk]
mustard	մանանեխ	[mana'neh]
non-alcoholic	ոչ ալկոհոլային	['votʃ alko:la'jın]
noodles	լափշա	[lap'ʃʌ]
oats	վարսակ	[var'sak]
olive oil	ձիթապտղի ձեթ	[dzitapt'hi 'dzet]
olives	ձեյթուն	[dzitap'tuh]

omelet	ձվածեղ	[ʤva'ʦeh]
onion	սոխ	[soh]
orange	նարինջ	[na'rinʤ]
orange juice	նարնջի հյութ	[narn'ʤi h'jut]
orange-cap boletus	կարմրագլուխ սունկ	[karmrag'luh 'suŋk]
oyster	ոստրե	[vost're]
pâté	պաշտետ	[paʃ'tet]
papaya	պապայա	[pa'paja]
paprika	պապրիկա	['paprika]
parsley	մաղադանոս	[mahada'nos]
pasta	մակարոն	[maka'ron]
pea	սիսեռ	[si'ser]
peach	դեղձ	[dehʣ]
peanut	գետնընկույզ	[getnı'ŋkujz]
pear	տանձ	[tanʣ]
peel	կլեպ	[klep]
perch	պերկես	[per'kes]
pickled	մարինացված	[marinaʦ'vaʦ]
pie	կարկանդակ	[karkan'dak]
piece	կտոր	[ktor]
pike	գայլաձուկ	[gajla'ʣuk]
pike perch	շիղաձուկ	[ʃiha'ʣuk]
pineapple	արքայախնձոր	[arkajahn'ʣor]
pistachios	պիստակ	[pis'tak]
pizza	պիցցա	['piʦa]
plate	ափսե	[ap'se]
plum	սալոր	[sa'lor]
poisonous mushroom	թունավոր սունկ	[tuna'vor 'suŋk]
pomegranate	նուռ	[nur]
pork	խոզի միս	[ho'zi 'mis]
porridge	շիլա	[ʃi'la]
portion	բաժին	[ba'ʒin]
potato	կարտոֆիլ	[karto'fil]
proteins	սպիտակուցներ	[spitakuʦ'ner]
pub, bar	բար	[bar]
pumpkin	դդում	[ddum]
rabbit	ճագար	[ʧa'gar]
radish	բողկ	[bohk]
raisin	չամիչ	[ʧa'miʧ]
raspberry	մորի	[mo'ri]
recipe	բաղադրատոմս	[bahadra'toms]
red pepper	կարմիր պղպեղ	[kar'mir ph'peh]
red wine	կարմիր գինի	[kar'mir gi'ni]
redcurrant	կարմիր հաղարջ	[kar'mir a'harʤ]
refreshing drink	զովացուցիչ ըմպելիք	[zovaʦu'ʦiʧ ımpe'lik]
rice	բրինձ	[brinʣ]
rum	ռոմ	[rom]
russula	դառնամատիտեղ	[darnamati'teh]
rye	տարեկան	[tare'kan]
saffron	շաֆրան	[ʃʌf'ran]
salad	աղցան	[ah'ʦan]
salmon	սաղման	[sah'man]

salt	աղ	[ah]
salty	աղի	[a'hi]
sandwich	բրդուճ	[brdutʃ]
sardine	սարդինա	[sar'dina]
sauce	սոուս	[so'us]
saucer	պնակ	[pnak]
sausage	երշիկ	[er'ʃik]
seafood	ծովամթերքներ	[tsovamterk'ner]
sesame	քնջութ	[kndʒut]
shark	շնաձուկ	[ʃna'dzuk]
shrimp	մանր ծովախեցգետին	['manr tsovahetsge'tin]
side dish	գառնիր	[gar'nir]
slice	պատառ	[pa'tar]
smoked	ապխտած	[aph'tats]
soft drink	ոչ ալկոհոլային ըմպելիք	['votʃ alko:la'jın ımpe'lik]
soup	ապուր	[a'pur]
soup spoon	ճաշի գդալ	[tʃaʃi g'dal]
sour cherry	բալ	[bal]
sour cream	թթվասեր	[ttva'ser]
soy	սոյա	[so'ja]
spaghetti	սպագետի	[spa'getti]
sparkling	գազով	[ga'zov]
spice	համեմունք	[ame'muŋk]
spinach	սպինատ	[spi'nat]
spiny lobster	լանգուստ	[la'ŋust]
spoon	գդալ	[gdal]
squid	կաղամար	[kaha'mar]
steak	բիֆշտեքս	[bifʃ'teks]
stew	տապակած միս	[tapa'kats 'mis]
still	առանց գազի	[a'rants ga'zi]
strawberry	ելակ	[e'lak]
sturgeon	թառափ	[ta'rap]
sugar	շաքար	[ʃʌ'kar]
sunflower oil	արևածաղկի ձեթ	[arevatsah'ki 'dzet]
sweet	քաղցր	[kahtsr]
sweet cherry	կեռաս	[ke'ras]
taste, flavor	համ	[am]
tasty	համեղ	[a'meh]
tea	թեյ	[tej]
teaspoon	թեյի գդալ	[tejı g'dal]
tip	թեյավճար	[teja'poh]
tomato	լոլիկ	[lo'lik]
tomato juice	տոմատի հյութ	[toma'ti h'jut]
tongue	լեզու	[le'zu]
toothpick	ատամնափորիչ	[atamnapo'ritʃ]
trout	իշխան	[iʃ'han]
tuna	թյունոս	[ty'ŋos]
turkey	հնդկահավ	[ındka'av]
turnip	շաղգամ	[ʃʌh'gam]
veal	հորթի միս	[or'ti 'mis]
vegetable oil	բուսական յուղ	[busa'kan 'juh]
vegetables	բանջարեղեն	[bandʒare'hen]

vegetarian	բուսակեր	[busa'ker]
vegetarian	բուսակերական	[busakera'kan]
vermouth	վերմուտ	['vermut]
vienna sausage	նրբերշիկ	[nrber'ʃik]
vinegar	քացախ	[ka'tsah]
vitamin	վիտամին	[vita'min]
vodka	օղի	[o'hi]
waffles	վաֆլի	[vaf'li]
waiter	մատուցող	[matu'tsoh]
waitress	մատուցողուհի	[matutsohu'i]
walnut	ընկույզ	[ı'ŋkujz]
water	ջուր	[ʤur]
watermelon	ձմերուկ	[dzme'ruk]
wheat	ցորեն	[tso'ren]
whisky	վիսկի	['viski]
white wine	սպիտակ գինի	[spi'tak gi'ni]
wine	գինի	[gi'ni]
wine list	գինիների գրացանկ	[ginine'ri gra'tsaŋk]
with ice	սառուցով	[saru'tsov]
yogurt	յոգուրտ	[jo'gurt]
zucchini	դդմիկ	[ddmik]

Armenian-English gastronomic glossary

Բարի՛ ախորժակ:	[ba'ri ahor'ʒak]	Enjoy your meal!
ազդր	[azdr]	gammon
ալկոհոլային խմիչքներ	[alko:la'jın hmitʃk'ner]	liquors
ալյուր	[a'lyr]	flour
ախորժակ	[ahor'ʒak]	appetite
ածխաջրեր	[atshadʒ'rer]	carbohydrates
աղ	[ah]	salt
աղանդեր	[ahan'der]	dessert
աղացած միս	[aha'tsats 'mis]	hamburger
աղի	[a'hi]	salty
աղցան	[ah'tsan]	salad
անիսոն	[ani'son]	anise
ապերիտիվ	[aperi'tiv]	aperitif
ապխտած	[aph'tats]	smoked
ապուր	[a'pur]	soup
առանց գազի	[a'rants ga'zi]	still
ավոկադո	[avo'kado]	avocado
ատամնափորիչ	[atamnapo'ritʃ]	toothpick
արմավ	[ar'mav]	date
արտիճուկ	[arti'tʃuk]	artichoke
արքայախնձոր	[arkajahn'dzor]	pineapple
արևածաղկի ձեթ	[arevatsah'ki 'dzet]	sunflower oil
ափսե	[ap'se]	plate
բադ	[bad]	duck
բազուկ	[ba'zuk]	beetroot
բաժակ	[ba'ʒak]	glass
բաժակ	[ba'ʒak]	cup
բաժին	[ba'ʒin]	portion
բալ	[bal]	sour cherry
բաղադրատոմս	[bahadra'toms]	recipe
բանան	[ba'nan]	banana
բանջարեղեն	[bandʒare'hen]	vegetables
բար	[bar]	pub, bar
բարմեն	[bar'men]	bartender
բաց գարեջուր	['bats gare'dʒur]	light beer
բացիչ	[ba'tsitʃ]	bottle opener
բացիչ	[ba'tsitʃ]	can opener
բեկոն	[be'kon]	bacon
բիֆշտեքս	[bifʃ'teks]	steak
բողկ	[bohk]	radish
բուսական յուղ	[busa'kan 'juh]	vegetable oil
բուսակեր	[busa'ker]	vegetarian
բուսակերական	[busakera'kan]	vegetarian
բրամ	[bram]	bream

բրդուճ	[brdutʃ]	sandwich
բրինձ	[brindz]	rice
բրյուսելյան կաղամբ	[bryse'ʎan ka'hamb]	Brussels sprouts
գազավորված	[gazavor'vats]	carbonated
գազար	[ga'zar]	carrot
գազոտ	[ga'zov]	sparkling
գայլաձուկ	[gajla'dzuk]	pike
գառնիր	[gar'nir]	side dish
գավաթ	[ga'vat]	glass
գարեջուր	[gare'dʒur]	beer
գարի	[ga'ri]	barley
գդալ	[gdal]	spoon
գետածածան	[getatsa'tsan]	carp
գետնընկույզ	[getnı'ŋkujz]	peanut
գինի	[gi'ni]	wine
գինիների գրացանկ	[ginine'ri gra'tsaŋk]	wine list
գինձ	[gindz]	coriander
գրեյպֆրուտ	[grejpf'rut]	grapefruit
դանակ	[da'nak]	knife
դառը	['darı]	bitter
դառնամատիտեղ	[darnamati'teh]	russula
դարչին	[dar'tʃin]	cinnamon
դափնու տերև	[dap'nu te'rev]	bay leaf
դդմիկ	[ddmik]	zucchini
դդում	[ddum]	pumpkin
դեղձ	[dehdz]	peach
դեղնուց	[deh'nuts]	egg yolk
եգիպտացորեն	[egiptatso'ren]	corn
եգիպտացորեն	[egiptatso'ren]	corn
եգիպտացորենի փաթիլներ	[egiptatsore'ni patil'ner]	cornflakes
ելակ	[e'lak]	strawberry
երշիկ	[er'ʃik]	sausage
եփած	[e'pats]	boiled
զեյթուն	[dzitap'tuh]	olives
զովացուցիչ ըմպելիք	[zovatsu'tsitʃ ımpe'lik]	refreshing drink
ընթրիք	[ınt'rik]	dinner
ընկույզ	[ı'ŋkujz]	walnut
թառափ	[ta'rap]	sturgeon
թարմ քամված հյութ	['tarm kam'vats h'jut]	freshly squeezed juice
թեյ	[tej]	tea
թեյավճար	[teja'poh]	tip
թեյի գդալ	[tejı g'dal]	teaspoon
թթվասեր	[ttva'ser]	sour cream
թխվածքաբլիթ	[thvatskab'lit]	cookies
թյունիկ	[ty'nik]	mackerel
թյունոս	[ty'ŋos]	tuna
թուզ	[tuz]	fig
թունավոր սունկ	[tuna'vor 'suŋk]	poisonous mushroom
թունավոր սունկ	[tuna'vor 'suŋk]	death cap
ժանտասունկ	[ʒanta'suŋk]	birch bolete
իմբիր	[im'birʲ]	ginger

իշխան	[iʃ'han]	trout
լանգուստ	[la'ŋust]	spiny lobster
լափշա	[lap'ʃʌ]	noodles
լեզու	[le'zu]	tongue
լիկյոր	[li'kзr]	liqueur
լիմոնադ	[limo'nad]	lemonade
լյարդ	[ʎard]	liver
լոբի	[lo'bi]	beans
լոբի	[lo'bi]	kidney bean
լոլիկ	[lo'lik]	tomato
լոռամրգի	[loramr'gi]	cranberry
լուծվող սուրճ	[luʦ'voh 'surʧ]	instant coffee
լոքո	[lo'ko]	catfish
լցոն	[lʦon]	filling
խաղող	[ha'hoh]	grape
խմելու ջուր	[hme'lu 'ʤur]	drinking water
խնձոր	[hnʣor]	apple
խոզապուխտ	[hoza'puht]	ham
խոզի միս	[ho'zi 'mis]	pork
խոհանոց	[hoa'noʦ]	cuisine
խորտիկ	[hor'tik]	appetizer
խտացրած կաթ	[htaʦ'raʦ 'kat]	condensed milk
խցանահան	[hʦana'an]	corkscrew
ծաղկակաղամբ	[ʦahkaka'hamb]	cauliflower
ծիրան	[ʦi'ran]	apricot
ծնեբեկ	[ʦne'bek]	asparagus
ծովաբողկ	[ʦova'bohk]	horseradish
ծովախեցգետին	[ʦovaheʦge'tin]	crab
ծովամթերքներ	[ʦovamterk'ner]	seafood
ծովատառեխ	[ʦovata'reh]	herring
կաթ	[kat]	milk
կաթնային կոկտեյլ	[katna'jɪn kok'tejʎ]	milkshake
կաթով սուրճ	[ka'tov 'surʧ]	coffee with milk
կալորիա	[ka'lorija]	calorie
կաղամար	[kaha'mar]	squid
կաղամբ	[ka'hamb]	cabbage
կաղամբ բրոկոլի	[ka'hamb bro'koli]	broccoli
կանաչ թեյ	[ka'naʧ 'tej]	green tea
կանաչի	[kana'ʧi]	greens
կարկանդակ	[karkan'dak]	pie
կարմիր գինի	[kar'mir gi'ni]	red wine
կարմիր հաղարջ	[kar'mir a'harʤ]	redcurrant
կարմիր պղպեղ	[kar'mir ph'peh]	red pepper
կարմրագլուխ սունկ	[karmrag'luh 'suŋk]	orange-cap boletus
կարտոֆիլ	[karto'fil]	potato
կարտոֆիլի պյուրե	[kartofi'li py're]	mashed potatoes
կեռաս	[ke'ras]	sweet cherry
կերակուր	[kera'kur]	food
կիվի	['kivi]	kiwi
կիտրոն	[kit'ron]	lemon
կլեպ	[klep]	peel
կոկոսի ընկույզ	[ko'kosi ɪ'ŋkujz]	coconut

կոկտեյլ	[kok'tejʎ]	cocktail
կողմնակի համ	[kohmnɑ'ki 'ɑm]	aftertaste
կոնյակ	[ko'ɲjɑk]	cognac
կոնֆետ	[kon'fet]	candy
կոտլետ	[kot'let]	fried meatballs
կորեկ	[ko'rek]	millet
կտոր	[ktor]	piece
կրեմ	[krem]	buttercream
հաղարջ	[ɑ'harʤ]	gooseberry
համ	[ɑm]	taste, flavor
համբուրգեր	[ɑmbur'ger]	hamburger
համեղ	[ɑ'meh]	tasty
համեմունք	[ɑme'muŋk]	condiment
համեմունք	[ɑme'muŋk]	spice
հանքային ջուր	[ɑŋkɑ'jɪn 'ʤur]	mineral water
հաշիվ	[ɑ'ʃiv]	check
հապալաս	[ɑpɑ'lɑs]	bilberry
հապալաս	[ɑpɑ'lɑs]	cowberry
հասկ	[ɑsk]	ear
հավ	[ɑv]	chicken
հատապտուղ	[ɑtɑp'tuh]	berry
հատապտուղներ	[ɑtɑptuh'ner]	berries
հաց	[hɑʦ]	bread
հացահատիկ	[ɑʦɑ:'tik]	grain
հացահատիկային բույսեր	[ɑʦɑ:tikɑ'jɪn buj'ser]	cereal crops
հյութ	[hjut]	juice
հնդկահավ	[ɪndkɑ'ɑv]	turkey
հնդկացորեն	[ɪndkɑʦo'ren]	buckwheat
հորթի միս	[or'ti 'mis]	veal
հրուշակ	[ɛru'ʃʌk]	cake
հրուշակեղեն	[ɛruʃʌke'hen]	confectionery
ձավար	[ʣɑ'vɑr]	cereal grains
ձիթապտղի ձեթ	[ʣitɑpt'hi 'ʣet]	olive oil
ձկնկիթ	[ʣkŋkit]	caviar
ձմերուկ	[ʣme'ruk]	watermelon
ձողաձուկ	[ʣohɑ'ʣuk]	cod
ձու	[ʣu]	egg
ձուկ	[ʣuk]	fish
ձվածեղ	[ʣvɑ'ʦeh]	fried eggs
ձվածեղ	[ʣvɑ'ʦeh]	omelet
ձվասունկ	[ʣvɑ'suŋk]	chanterelle
ձվեր	[ʣver]	eggs
ճագար	[ʧɑ'gɑr]	rabbit
ճանճասպան	[ʧɑnʧɑs'pɑn]	fly agaric
ճաշ	[ʧɑʃ]	lunch
ճաշատեսակ	[ʧɑʃʌte'sɑk]	course, dish
ճաշի գդալ	[ʧɑʃi g'dɑl]	soup spoon
ճարպեր	[ʧɑr'per]	fats
մակարոն	[mɑkɑ'ron]	pasta
մաղադանոս	[mɑhɑdɑ'nos]	parsley
մայոնեզ	[mɑjo'nez]	mayonnaise
մանանեխ	[mɑnɑ'neh]	mustard

մանգո	['maŋo]	mango
մանդարին	[manda'rin]	mandarin
մանր ծովախեցգետին	['manr tsovahetsge'tin]	shrimp
մաստակ	[mas'tak]	chewing gum
մատուցող	[matu'tsoh]	waiter
մատուցողուհի	[matutsohu'i]	waitress
մարգարին	[marga'rin]	margarine
մարինացված	[marinats'vats]	pickled
մարմելադ	[marme'lad]	marmalade
մեխակ	[me'hak]	cloves
մեղր	[mehr]	honey
մենյու	[me'ny]	menu
միս	[mis]	meat
միրգ	[mirg]	fruit
մոշ	[moʃ]	blackberry
մորի	[mo'ri]	raspberry
մորխ	[morh]	morel
մուգ գարեջուր	['mug gare'dʒur]	dark beer
մուրաբա	[mura'ba]	jam
մսաջուր	[msa'dʒur]	clear soup
յոգուրտ	[jo'gurt]	yogurt
նախաճաշ	[naha'tʃaʃ]	breakfast
նարինջ	[na'rindʒ]	orange
նարնջի հյութ	[narn'dʒi h'jut]	orange juice
նեխուր	[ne'hur]	celery
նուշ	[nuʃ]	almond
նուռ	[nur]	pomegranate
նրբերշիկ	[nrber'ʃik]	vienna sausage
շաղգամ	[ʃʌh'gam]	turnip
շամպայն	[ʃʌm'pajn]	champagne
շաքար	[ʃʌ'kar]	sugar
շաֆրան	[ʃʌf'ran]	saffron
շիլա	[ʃi'la]	porridge
շիղաձուկ	[ʃiha'dzuk]	pike perch
շնաձուկ	[ʃna'dzuk]	shark
շոկոլադ	[ʃoko'lad]	chocolate
շոկոլադե	[ʃokola'dɛ]	chocolate
ոչ ալկոհոլային	['votʃ alko:la'jın]	non-alcoholic
ոչ ալկոհոլային ըմպելիք	['votʃ alko:la'jın ımpe'lik]	soft drink
ոչխարի միս	[votʃha'ri 'mis]	lamb
ոսպ	[vosp]	lentil
ոստրե	[vost're]	oyster
որսամիս	[vorsa'mis]	game
ուտելու սունկ	[ute'lu 'suŋk]	edible mushroom
չաման	[tʃa'man]	caraway
չամիչ	[tʃa'mitʃ]	raisin
չորացրած	[tʃorats'rats]	dried
պահածոներ	[pa:tso'ner]	canned food
պաղպաղակ	[pahpa'hak]	ice-cream
պանիր	[pa'nir]	cheese
պաշտետ	[paʃ'tet]	pâté
պապայա	[pa'paja]	papaya

պապրիկա	['paprika]	paprika
պատառ	[pa'tar]	slice
պատառաքաղ	[patara'kah]	fork
պերկես	[per'kes]	perch
պիստակ	[pis'tak]	pistachios
պիցցա	['pitsa]	pizza
պղպեղ	[phpeh]	bell pepper
պնակ	[pnak]	saucer
պնդուկ	[pnduk]	hazelnut
ջեմ	[dʒem]	jam
ջին	[dʒin]	gin
ջուր	[dʒur]	water
ռեհան	[re'han]	basil
ռոմ	[rom]	rum
սագ	[sag]	goose
սալ	[sal]	lard
սալաթ	[sa'lat]	lettuce
սալոր	[sa'lor]	plum
սաղման	[sah'man]	salmon
սաղման ձուկ	[sah'man 'dzuk]	Atlantic salmon
սամիթ	[sa'mit]	dill
սառեցված	[sarets'vats]	frozen
սառը	['sarı]	cold
սառույց	[sa'rujts]	ice
սառուցով	[saru'tsov]	with ice
սարդինա	[sar'dina]	sardine
սեխ	[seh]	melon
սերուցք	[se'rutsk]	cream
սերուցքային կարագ	[serutska'jın ka'rag]	butter
սերուցքով սուրճ	[seruts'kov 'surtʃ]	cappuccino
սիսեռ	[si'ser]	pea
սխտոր	[shtor]	garlic
սմբուկ	[smbuk]	eggplant
սննդակարգ	[sŋda'karg]	diet
սոխ	[soh]	onion
սոյա	[so'ja]	soy
սոուս	[so'us]	sauce
սունկ	[suŋk]	mushroom
սուրճ	[surtʃ]	coffee
սպագետի	[spa'getti]	spaghetti
սպինատ	[spi'nat]	spinach
սպիտակ գինի	[spi'tak gi'ni]	white wine
սպիտակ սունկ	[spi'tak 'suŋk]	cep
սպիտակուց	[spita'kuts]	egg white
սպիտակուցներ	[spitakuts'ner]	proteins
սև թեյ	[sev 'tej]	black tea
սև հաղարջ	['sev a'hardʒ]	blackcurrant
սև պղպեղ	[sev ph'peh]	black pepper
սև սուրճ	[sev 'surtʃ]	black coffee
վահանաձուկ	[va:na'dzuk]	halibut
վայրի ելակ	[vaj'ri e'lak]	field strawberry
վարունգ	[va'ruŋ]	cucumber

վարսակ	[var'sak]	oats
վաֆլի	[vaf'li]	waffles
վերմուտ	['vermut]	vermouth
վիսկի	['viski]	whisky
վիտամին	[vita'min]	vitamin
տանձ	[tandz]	pear
տապակած	[tapa'kats]	fried
տապակած միս	[tapa'kats 'mis]	stew
տավարի միս	[tava'ri 'mis]	beef
տարեկան	[tare'kan]	rye
տափակաձուկ	[tapaka'dzuk]	flatfish
տաք	[tak]	hot
տոմատի հյութ	[toma'ti h'jut]	tomato juice
տորթ	[tort]	cake
ցորեն	[tso'ren]	wheat
փշուր	[pʃur]	crumb
քաղցր	[kahtsr]	sweet
քացախ	[ka'tsah]	vinegar
քնջութ	[kndʒut]	sesame
օձաձուկ	[odza'dzuk]	eel
օղի	[o'hi]	vodka

23845446R00119

Printed in Poland
by Amazon Fulfillment
Poland Sp. z o.o., Wrocław